Praise for

THE EVERYDAY COACH

Harnessing the Magic of Influence

"Everyone is a coach, every day, in every aspect of their life. Harrison provides a refreshing approach to improve our relationships in everyday life through the experiences of the best coaches in the world."

—Martin Rooney, Founder, Training for Warriors; internationally recognized coach, fitness expert, and bestselling author of ***Coach to Coach***

"Harrison showcases his deep understanding of effective coaching to build championship teams."

—Jon Torine, NFL strength and conditioning coach for 16 years (1995-2011), Buffalo Bills and Indianapolis Colts; founder, Lean In Coaching

"A rigorous, compelling and practical compendium drawing from the experiences of business, sports, and military leaders. A must read for every leader and coach inspiring and molding everyday people into competitive athletes and winning teams. Harrison Bernstein's inspirational and practical approach will guide aspiring and current coaches to fulfill their vision of success and winning."

—Major General John Uberti, U.S. Army (ret.), global executive and team builder, Raytheon; previously former Deputy Commanding General for Support, U.S. Army Installation Management Command; former Chief of Staff, United States Strategic Command

"Harrison highlights the most influential concepts in building team culture and personnel development in *The Everyday Coach*. Many of these ideas I incorporate every day into my coaching practice. Proper culture provides the best opportunities for personal development for everyone in your program."

—**Gregg Williams, 30+ year NFL Head Coach and Defensive Coordinator**

"Am I walking the talk? *The Everyday Coach* reminds us we owe people the same intention, attitude and effort we expect from them. Always. Learning can be messy, and success is not linear. Coaches that embrace this philosophy communicate differently with the people and teams they lead. The chapters in this book offer ingredients reflective of a mastery environment, one where mistakes are evaluated as growth opportunities and where effort is praised over outcomes. When people form a new relationship with failure, increases in motivation and perseverance are healthy by-products. This book is an awesome reminder that while winning matters, it's only one way we can evaluate success."

—**Ben Freakly, Jr., Head of Mental Performance, MLB Toronto Blue Jays; founder of Ready. Set. Resilient, a sport and performance psychology consultancy aimed at helping individuals and teams optimize performance**

"I wish I could go back 25 years and teach myself the coaching lessons we discuss in *The Everyday Coach*. Influencing players and coaches to be the best version of themselves is the secret to leadership success. This book will show you the way."

—**Matt Doherty, former Head Basketball Coach, University of North Carolina, University of Notre Dame, Florida Atlantic University and Southern Methodist University**

"In an increasingly complex world, *The Everyday Coach* is a must-read handbook that illuminates the need for conscious leadership for youth sports and beyond."

—Perry Jobe Smith, Founder of Minute Man Restaurants and The Avalon Institute

"Harrison has spent most of his adult life studying how to help improve people's lives through exercise, sports, and positive mental health. *The Everyday Coach* is a must read for parents, coaches, athletes and anyone interested in learning how to set goals, work hard and excel at whatever path you choose in life."

—William C. MacDonald, CEO, President, Mill Creek Residential Trust

"Many of the best leadership lessons I learned and used throughout my military career I learned from coaches, including the great Vince Lombardi. They are discussed in this book in a profoundly entertaining way. A must read for coaches and leaders."

—General George Casey, Jr., U.S. Army (ret.), Chairman, USO Board of Governors; 36th Chief of Staff of the United States Army (2007–2011); Commanding General, Multi-National Force - Iraq (2004–2007)

"*The Everyday Coach* highlights several of the best methods to achieve an inspiring and motivating company culture of high performance."

—Jack Talley, Vice President, Enterprise Fleet Management, Enterprise Rent-A-Car

"*The Everyday Coach* and the man behind it offer a unique but simple way to approach managing life and the development and growth that makes life both challenging and satisfying. Over the years of working with the materials in this book, both in a professional and personal manner, I find myself returning to the core principles and teachings when in need. They stand the true test of time as remaining relevant and fulfilling when you apply them to life. Truly, this book and its author are an inspiration on an EVERYDAY level."

—Josh Grapski, Managing Partner, La Vida Hospitality

"I have had the honor of participating in several outstanding Soldiers To Sidelines seminars and sessions, and know that Harrison and this effort are making a difference in veterans' lives. All of us search for meaning, purpose, and another form of service once we take off the uniform, and Soldiers To Sidelines offers a clear path: coaching. That path should be obvious to every veteran but it is often not considered or is thought to be out of our reach. Harrison proves how wrong we are! What you will find here is a combination of leadership and management instruction, a touch of self-help, and a strong dose of how-to. It is delivered with empathy by someone who knows the value of great coaching and wants to share his knowledge with veterans and non-veterans alike."

—Major General Tony Cucolo, U.S. Army (ret.); previously the Army's Chief of Public Affairs; Commander, 3rd Infantry Division and Fort Stewart/Hunter Army Airfield (GA); Commandant, Army War College

"*The Everyday Coach* is a book with so many relevant messages that will resonate with coaches and athletes at all levels. Coaching with confidence, building players up, and learning to grow are essential for any team, and each of these is highlighted in unique ways throughout. These lessons are not just for coaches or athletes, but are applicable to any leader who influences people in a team setting. I would recommend this book for anyone looking for renewed energy and motivation in these key areas."

—Greg Chimera, Head Football Coach, Johns Hopkins University

THE EVERYDAY COACH

Harnessing the Magic of Influence

HARRISON BERNSTEIN

FOREWORD BY COACH MACK BROWN
HEAD FOOTBALL COACH
UNIVERSITY OF NORTH CAROLINA

The Everyday Coach: Harnessing the Magic of Influence

Published by
The Everyday Coach Group
17461 Taramino Place
Lewes, DE 19958

Cover design:
Natalie Wunn
www.99designs.com

Interior design:
Clark Kenyon
www.camppope.com

Illustrations:
Alvaré Design
Pace, FL

ISBN: 979-8-5791-1817-2 (Paperback)

Printed in the United States of America

DEDICATION

The Everyday Coach is dedicated to three coaches who profoundly impacted me and the Soldiers To Sidelines mission.

First and foremost, I dedicate this book to my mother, Bernadette DeLong (1950–2020). She championed a mindset for me that I could accomplish anything with hard work and dedication. She instilled my belief that living for purpose greater than self is the true meaning of life. I love you and will miss you forever.

Next, Jim Margraff (1960–2019), my college football coach, who set THE example of how to lead with the highest standards of integrity. He was patient, strict, and caring during my most boneheaded moments. I am forever grateful. Your legacy will live forever among all of the champions you have coached. Pride and Poise!

Finally, Bill Starr (1938–2015), my college strength and conditioning coach, filled us with great belief in our ultimate potential. He is the reason I pursued Sports Performance Coaching after college and is the impetus for my entire career. His wisdom and teachings live in perpetuity in all of Soldiers To Sidelines actions and words. Today he roams with the white buffalo, ready to flash before our eyes in our toughest and biggest moments. His spirit gives us strength.

FOREWORD

As coaches and as leaders, we have a common purpose. What is that purpose? To educate, mentor, and help people learn how to handle whatever is next.

Transitions are tough, but there are principles you've learned through your unique life experience that have put you in a position to help people. What I've learned is first, you must be fair, and do the fair thing for everyone. Second, be consistent – consistency is being who we are every day, so give the gift of consistency. And third, do what you know is right.

You already know what the right thing is. It's why you're reading this book. You already have what it takes to be a successful coach, because you know this: when someone is struggling, you don't beat them down, you lift them up.

If you're going to coach, coach because you want to help people. Coach to be a mentor. Coach to help people have a better life. You know what it means to be accountable to the people on your right and on your left, so take that experience and instill it in others.

We need people like you as coaches, people with good hearts who care about making a difference and love the game. You're being asked to help young people grow and win. They're asking you to help them learn the traits of a successful person. As a coach once said to me, if you quit, you lose. If you keep fighting during a game, but you come up short, you didn't lose, you just ran out of time.

One of the greatest joys in my life is people coming back to me years later, long after I've coached them. They remember what we say to them. They appreciate and use the life lessons we as coaches provide. My wife said it to me once, and I am now saying it to you: this is your gift, to reach out and help people. This is your next opportunity: understanding what it means to be a coach, and using your gifts to lift up the people around you.

Coach Mack Brown
Head Football Coach
University of North Carolina
11 November 2020

CREATE
realize our 'why'

Culture · Communication
C.A.R.E. · Technique
Strategy · Preparation
Environment

CONVEY
remember our 'why'

Fun · Knowledge
Message · Scars
Candor · Fitness

COMPEL
redefine our 'why'

·Inspiration
·Motivation

Failure = Get your **MISSES** up

FAILURE

TABLE OF CONTENTS

PART 3 CONVEY - REMEMBERING AND PROMOTING OUR "WHY"   67

PART 4 CREATE - REALIZING OUR "WHY"   111

A NOTE FROM THE AUTHOR

Imagine you're in an inviting, beautifully appointed owners' space inside a professional sports facility. The carpets and furnishings are magnificently plush and comfortable. The temperature and lighting are perfect. A wall of windows overlooks the field below. Other walls are richly layered with one-of-a-kind memorabilia, signed photos, trophies, and original artwork representing championships, milestones, icons, and legacies. It is a rare and sacred space.

A carefully curated group of guests gathers, many greeting each other like the old friends they are. They represent a wide spectrum of industries, professions, experiences, and accomplishments. Over a feast of elegant food and craft beverages, the animated conversations flow easily, peppered with laughter and energy.

After dinner, the subject turns to coaching. Regardless of background or profession, everyone has something to contribute to the conversation, and something to learn as well. This book echoes such events, and I hope you find yourself both contributing to and learning from the conversation unfolding within these pages.

Harrison

PART 1

~~FAILURE~~
MISS

– And why it isn't final

PROLOGUE

My shins are bleeding, my thumb knuckles are raw, and my collar bone is blurple. Blurple is a purple so deep it's black. I've been standing on this Olympic weightlifting platform in my college weight room for just about an hour, chasing an elusive personal record in the power clean.

My coach is a 61-year-old wise man named Bill Starr, considered a legend in strength and conditioning. He was a former strength coach for the Baltimore Colts, author of one of the most famous strength and conditioning books ever written, *The Strongest Shall Survive*, and a veteran of the United States Air Force. Now he's here at Johns Hopkins University, limping over to me after finishing his 5 rep squat set of 365 lbs. to offer some advice on how I can achieve my personal record.

For the past three weeks, I have been able to power clean 305 lbs. from the floor to my chest without the assistance of straps, wraps, or any other equipment. However, I've been missing 315 by a narrow margin each week as well. This frustrates me greatly, and I'm beginning to feel like it's impossible. Maybe I'm just not that strong, and I need to accept that fact.

Between his squat sets, Starrman has been watching me miss every attempt at 315 and taking note of every error I make. He gets to my platform and says, "I see you have been struggling with 315 for a while now." I nod in confirmation and express my frustration because I feel like I'm so close to getting it. He looks me dead in the eye and tells me to attempt 365 for three sets of one rep. "Are you serious?" I ask. "If I can't get 315, what makes you think I can get 365?!" Starrman insists I just give it my best effort and see how it goes.

As you can imagine, each attempt at 365 is an exhausting failure. Here he comes again and rhetorically asks how it went. I tell him my traps and back are on fire. "Take a five minute break, get some water and black coffee, and return to the platform to attempt another set at a lighter weight of 275." Bill Starr has spent three years coaching me, and I hang on every word he says. I comply.

Five minutes later, the 275 lb. bar launches off the platform to my chest as if the bar lifted itself. "Wow! That felt good!" I exclaim. With that, he says, "Take another two minutes and try 315 once more," and pokes me in the chest with his sharpened pinky nail. A droplet of blood slowly leaks through my shirt. He has a unique way of motivating me.

I have been power cleaning in the gym for an hour and a half and I'm growing weary. I address the 315 lb. bar and go through my standard procedure setup. My vision narrows and I squeeze the bar so tight water is about to come out of the steel. I pull the bar from the floor and make the most explosive jump I can muster. The bar shoots vertically and somehow lands on top of my chest. I'm astounded that after all this work and being completely worn out, I'm able to attain my personal record. Bill Starr simply looks at me and says, "Harrison, you've always had the strength… you just needed to get your misses up."

CHAPTER 1

KELSEY'S STORY

In high school, Kelsey was the best athlete in her class. She was honored as Female Student Athlete of the Year, earning 1st team All-State Honors in both softball and field hockey while carrying a GPA of 3.9. She was speedy, confident, aggressive, and consistently made acrobatic catches. Not surprisingly, she was heavily recruited to play Division 1 college softball and field hockey.

During one game, Kelsey was playing center field against a rival opponent in the state tournament. Her team was up 10-0 in the bottom of the fourth inning, and the opposing team had a runner on second base with two outs. This was clearly a blowout. However, if a team was up by 10 runs at the end of the 4th inning, they would win by slaughter rule and proceed to the final four.

The opposition had their best hitter at the plate and smashed a 5-foot high screaming line drive into the right center gap. Kelsey got a great jump on the ball, sprinted and launched her body parallel to the ground to make the game-winning catch.

A couple of days later, Kelsey found herself standing in center field in the 10th inning of the semi-final game of the tournament with two outs, a runner on third base, and her team up by one run. Earlier in the game, in the top of the inning, Kelsey scored the go-ahead run. Now her team was hanging on by a thread to preserve the lead and win the game that would send them to the championship.

It had already been a long game, and Kelsey's team had only given up one hit. In those kinds of pitcher duels, it was difficult but crucial to maintain alertness as an outfielder. Suddenly the opposing batter hit a bomb deep into center field, appearing to be a certain walk-off home run to win the game. Kelsey spun and sprinted backward to the wall, tracking the yellow dot soaring above the lights. Because the ball was hit so high, it rapidly spiraled downward just inside the fence. Kelsey lunged and extended her glove to the wall, making the game-winning catch to advance her team to the championship.

In college, Kelsey decided to play softball instead of field hockey, and accepted a scholarship offer to a beautiful school in the Southern Conference. Just before arriving on campus, she was told by her coach that her scholarship had been transferred to another recruit, but she could still be on the team as a non-scholarship walk-on. Just a couple of months away from moving to the new school, Kelsey's other scholarship offers had lapsed since she committed. Hurt by the sudden change, but now even more determined to prove her worth, she decided to attend this school anyway and prove her ability.

As a sophomore, she began to get more playing time in a pivotal growth period of her collegiate softball career. Early in the season, Kelsey was playing right field with a runner on second base in the third inning. The batter hit a low line drive, similar to the hit in the gap in her high school tournament. Kelsey charged forward, slid, and extended her glove against the ground, but this time the ball squirted behind her and the runner scored. At the end of the inning her coach pulled her from the game for "taking a reckless risk."

Despite this devastating blow to Kelsey's confidence, she was determined to work even harder. She began to increase her production in the batter's box, getting into a hitting streak for five straight games. Once again, while she was standing in right field with a runner on first base with two outs, a fast, choppy ground ball broke through the infield. Kelsey charged the ball. As she approached, she remembered the previous repercussions from her coach about taking risks. She safely blocked the ball with her chest, picked it up and returned it to the infield, preventing extra bases, but not getting the force out at second base. After the inning, once again, the coach pulled her from the game.

Dejected and confused, Kelsey later requested a meeting with her coach and asked why she kept getting pulled from the game. Her coach looked at her and said, "You can't handle pressure!" Her coach set the precedent that Kelsey shouldn't try to make plays, but shouldn't play it safe either. No matter what, the coach had decided Kelsey couldn't handle pressure.

With her playing time reduced, Kelsey began to doubt her decision-making skills. She anticipated a negative outcome to any decision – more yelling, more benching, less playing time – and her confidence as a player shrank.

During practice, Kelsey's coach would ask, "Why can't you play like that in the game? You're great in practice, but we don't know what you'll do in the game." Kelsey thought, but never said, "Because I know what happens when things don't go the way you expect!"

What did Kelsey need most? She needed her coach to believe in her and support her when she made an effort-based miss. Kelsey was getting her misses up, and her coach was putting her down. The coach lost a valuable opportunity to coach confidence in one player. The other players witnessed it, and the entire team lost all respect for their coach. To this day, the wounds from that coach's decisions have left a scar on Kelsey.

CHAPTER 2

WHAT IS FAILURE?

From birth, we're preparing to fail. Think about a baby's earliest attempts to walk. Those first lurching, awkward staggers inevitably land in fall after fall, over and over again. Yet the baby persists, pulling up again and again, and eventually they learn to coordinate balance, momentum, and direction for a few seconds, taking a few hesitant steps forward. And then they fall again. But eventually, they master the lifelong skill of walking effortlessly.

The Merriam-Webster dictionary defines failure as "a lack of success in some effort." Plans fail. Organs fail. Structures fail. Businesses fail. Crops fail. And we fail in our attempts to achieve success. Does that mean we are failures? No. It means our attempts failed.

- Thomas Edison's teachers told him he was "too stupid to learn anything." After that, things stayed bleak for a while, as Edison went on to be fired from his first two jobs for not being suitably productive. Edison went on to hold more than 1,000 patents and invented some world-changing devices, including the phonograph, practical electrical lamp, and movie camera.

- A young Henry Ford ruined his reputation with a couple of failed automobile businesses. However, after conducting a search, he was finally able to find a partner who had faith in him. Ford proved he had learned from his mistakes when Ford Motor Company forever changed the automotive industry and culture with his assembly line mode of production.

- Theodor Seuss Geisel, better known as Dr. Seuss, had his first book rejected by 27 different publishers. Dr. Seuss became a legendary children's author known around the world for classics like *The Cat in the Hat* and *Green Eggs and Ham*. His books have sold over 600 million copies.

- After Harrison Ford's first small movie role, an executive took him into his office and told him he'd never succeed in the movie business. Ford's career went on to span six decades, and has included timeless starring roles in blockbuster films like the *Star Wars* and *Indiana Jones* series.[1]

* * * * *

What do these four individuals have in common? None of them let their failures define their identity. In fact, Thomas Edison was later quoted as saying, "I have not failed. I've just found 10,000 ways that won't work."

Anticipating failure erodes, wearing us down like a river erodes rocks or constant waves erode shorelines. Conversely, expecting success builds us up and inspires growth and improvement. We can pick ourselves up. Here's how.

CHAPTER 3

FAILURE REDEFINED

We can start by redefining failure. Is it actual failure, or a fear of failing, that we're afraid of? We need to be clear, and redefine or reframe where necessary. Clarifying our definitions of failure and success can free us to see things in a different way.[2]

We've heard the term "failing forward." What does that really mean? Seeing our effort, whether we succeed or not, as our teacher, and the resulting success or failure bringing us the unique gifts of experience and lessons learned.

What if, instead of seeing failure as a measure of our worth, we recognized it as a chance for a new start? With that in mind, how would failure affect our goals?

We learn to be afraid to fail. How does fear of failure show up in our lives, and in the lives of our people?

> "Clarifying our definitions of failure and success can free us to see things in a different way."
> – Susan Peppercorn

- Reluctance to try new things or get involved in challenging projects

- Self-sabotage: procrastination, excessive anxiety or failure to follow through with goals

- Low self esteem or self confidence: negative statements like "I'm not good enough" or "I'm not smart enough"

- Perfectionism: a willingness to try only things we know we can do perfectly and successfully[3]

In her book *Being Wrong*, Katherine Schultz points out that we are wrong far more often than we're right. Of the things we know, how much do we know with 100% certainty? We live in a state of perpetually being wrong. With that in mind, we want to help our people understand that it's okay to be wrong, and to mitigate the *feeling* of being wrong. Being right feels so good, but the reality is, on some level, we're often wrong. Humility is being okay with being wrong.

At some point, we will do something wrong. We learn by trial and error. We don't learn by not making a choice or choosing a plan of action. Even choosing not to decide is a decision. Having the courage to be wrong, and encouraging failure in ourselves and others, is part of the journey toward getting better at whatever we're undertaking. I know that sounds very strange. When our SELF is the center of our focus, the feeling of being right is validating, and the feeling of failure is crushing. That feeling actually stems from our earliest need for self-preservation. Being right is our ego's favorite drug, and we will go to great lengths to get it.

Being right is our ego's favorite drug, and we will go to great lengths to get it.

Motivated by a fear of failure. Consider the recent college admission scandal involving two notable Hollywood figures and their daughters. Both were discovered making false claims, in one case faking standardized college placement test scores and in the other claiming phony athletic involvement. Both cases resulted in unwanted publicity, criminal charges, and long-term negative associations for both families. We can say, as parents, they had the right motives because they wanted to help their kids get into the best schools. And we would be wrong, because their choices were not based on what was best for their kids. Their choices came from a place of fear. They were fearful they would look like bad parents, because they didn't raise their kids to be smart enough to do what it took to get into the best schools. Fear of looking like failures as parents motivated them to manipulate the system to give their kids a competitive advantage.

Fear keeps us from acting with confidence. Fear blinds us. It causes us to make bad decisions. As everyday coaches, one of the best things we can do for our people is not just tell them, but show them what failing forward really looks like. One time, in a gathering of friends when we were cliff diving, I said, "Talk is bullsh#t when you're standing at the edge of a cliff and it's time to jump."

We only hear about this in retrospect. As everyday coaches, we need to know what fear looks like when we're facing it, and we need our own coaches to walk us through the darkness. When someone helps us face that fear of failure before we take that step forward, and tells us about it from their perspective before we fail, not after, we can learn from their experience as well as their wisdom.

Approach and avoidance. There are two types of goals: approach goals and avoidance goals. Approach goals move us toward a positive outcome, and avoidance goals steer us away from a negative outcome.[4] Sometimes we set goals based on what we don't want to happen rather than what we do want to happen. Author and investor Tim Ferriss suggests fear-setting, defining our nightmare, envisioning the absolute worst that could happen if we did what we are considering.[5]

For example, in a blog post entitled "Fear Setting: The Most Valuable Exercise I Do Every Month," Tim Ferriss says,

Why don't I decide exactly what my nightmare would be—the worst thing that could possibly happen as a result of my trip? Well, my business could fail while I'm overseas, for sure. Probably would. A legal warning letter would accidentally not get forwarded and I would get sued. My business would be shut down, and inventory would spoil on the shelves while I'm picking my toes in solitary misery on some cold shore in Ireland. Crying in the rain, I imagine. My bank account would crater by 80% and certainly my car and motorcycle in storage would be stolen. I suppose someone would probably spit on my head from a high-rise balcony while I'm feeding food scraps to a stray dog, which would then spook and bite me squarely on the face.[6]

Think about this. All of the fears on that fear-setting list are made up. They did not happen, and there's no guarantee they ever will. Instead of listing our fears in painstaking detail, giving them power by focusing our attention and energy on them, what if we turn that energy toward eradicating all fear, even fear of injury and death, and imagine what we *can* do? We would become supremely powerful.

How do we overcome that fear? Instead of focusing only on setting goals, consider listing, acknowledging, and addressing our fears, *including the fact that the fear is made up.*

Giving fear less power = fear less. An often-repeated Delta Force phrase says, "There are no bad decisions, there are only consequences." Fear is contrived, and death and injury are consequences. Fear is not a part of this equation, because from this perspective, decisions must be made based on a new set of circumstances, regardless of how we feel.

Assume positive intent. "Nobody gets up in the morning and says, 'I'm going to make a list of all the things I can do wrong today,'" says Major General John Uberti. General Uberti, U.S. Army (ret.), is a global executive and team builder for Raytheon; he previously served as former Deputy

Commanding General for Support, U.S. Army Installation Management Command, and former Chief of Staff, United States Strategic Command before his military retirement in 2018. "Assume positive intent until someone gives you cause or reason to doubt it. At that point, we should assess whether the cause or reason we're given is actually credible."

"Life will test you," says Cedric King, U.S. Army (ret.) Master Sergeant and double leg amputee who became a motivational speaker and author of *The Making Point*. "You will make mistakes. Don't give up. Keep practicing. Be the person you say you are."

CHAPTER 4

FAILURE'S ESSENTIAL ROLE

What drives our decisions? Several different influences, some internal and others external.

1. *Fear* of the past or the future. These decisions are driven by our minds, and none of our fears are 100% true.

2. *Others' influence.* This occurs when we give our decision-making power to other people.

3. *Logic.* Decisions based only on logic can leave us feeling flat, unenthusiastic, and wanting to hold on to control. No heart is involved in these decisions.

4. *Intuition.* Intuition is based on metadata that is collected beyond our conscious awareness. Nevertheless, it is important information that can provide deep context to logic. Intuitive choices are based on our heart. The key to making intuition-based decisions is to search for answers within ourselves. While it may be necessary to gather enough facts to make an informed decision, our intuition knows when we have what we need to make the right choice for us. Intuition-based decisions are the stuff of flow, ease, and miracles.[7]

"Crash and Learn." General George Casey, Jr. served as 36th Chief of Staff of the United States Army, April 2007–April 2011. He was Commanding General, Multi-National Force – Iraq, June 2004–February 2007. General Casey was in the Army his entire adult working life. He relates, "When I was a lieutenant in my first platoon, I screwed something up. I told my commander I was going to tell my men. He said, 'You can never let them know you screwed up.' I said, 'Why? They know it!'"

Later, I worked on the advisory board of a company tasked with making fuel tanks that didn't explode in a fire. Their mantra: 'crash and learn.' They'd conduct a test, and it wouldn't come out the way they wanted. Did they fail? No, they learned something! It's not about failing, it's about learning. We all have things that don't come out the way we want. The failure is if we don't learn from those things. Bad things happen to good organizations. If you don't get better from them, that's the real failure.

How can we take strategic risks and not be scared to miss? Try to assuage the fear of failure while letting people have the agency to miss.

Feeling of being right vs. feeling of being wrong. We aren't scared to fail. We're afraid of the feeling of failure. When we think we're right, that feels great. When we find out we're wrong, that feels horrible. Take risks! Don't be afraid to miss. We are wrong far more often than we're right, so we should at least have courage in the face of being wrong to try and get it more right the next time.

All of us have things that don't come out the way we want them to. Take those things and learn from them. Learn to differentiate the feeling of being right from the feeling of being wrong.

After-action review. It's actually helpful when we have to deal with failure, what we did wrong, and how we can do better. Feeling safe enough to talk about these things is integral to our relationships.

According to General Casey, the after-action review process did more to save the Army than anything else. "It came out of the early 1980s after a bad decade in the '70s with Vietnam," he says. "The whole purpose of the after-action review was critiquing ourselves. As battalion commander, I started it off, saying 'Here's where I think I screwed this up.' And that gave others courage to be candid. Everybody knows their piece."

We're not going to win every game or succeed the first time. As everyday coaches, speaking candidly about what we did wrong and what others did wrong is all part of getting better, feeling safe enough in that environment that we can talk about what we didn't do well without fear of retribution. There's an element of safety in that.

Knowledge and risk: George Washington's plan. Consider this: the entire reason the United States of America exists today is because George Washington suffered from smallpox as a teen. When Washington was a teenager suffering from tuberculosis, his wealthy brother took him to the Caribbean to help him recover. While there, young George contracted smallpox, a life-threatening disease with a high mortality rate, sometimes as high as 50%, meaning one out of every two people died from smallpox. Although permanently scarred by the horrific smallpox rash, Washington survived. He had no idea how his illness and recovery would affect not only his own future, but the future of our entire country.

In 1776, as commander of the Continental Army, Washington witnessed a seven-year outbreak of smallpox decimating his army. The British Army intentionally sent people infected with smallpox into Washington's camp trying to destroy the Continental Army and kill Washington. Unknown to the British, Washington's adolescent recovery from smallpox gave him lifelong immunity from the primitive biological warfare.

Armed with this knowledge, Washington took a tremendous risk. He knew trying to avoid exposure to smallpox wasn't an option. Instead, he decided to prevent its spread. At that time, vaccines were new and risky, and the smallpox vaccine was outlawed by the Continental Congress. Washington required his troops to be vaccinated against the disease, keeping this a secret from British forces to prevent them from attacking while his troops recovered from the vaccine's side effects. By the end of 1777, 40,000 troops were immune from smallpox, and they were able to focus on the real enemy: the British.[8]

Changing the future. According to the *Beastie Boys Story* documentary, when asked by a reporter if he was hypocritical because he once sang songs like "Girls" and "Fight For Your Right To Party" and later became a human rights advocate, lead singer Adam Yauch responded, "I'd rather be a hypocrite than the same person forever."

We have to allow room for change in our own lives and in the lives of those around us. In the 1999 movie *Magnolia*, there is a particularly memorable scene at the end of the movie when frogs begin falling from the sky. Up until that point, the characters in the movie experience what seem to be unfixable, unresolvable, deeply painful situations. When the frogs begin to fall, the event is completely unexplainable, yet the characters discover, this is real, and this is happening. They also discover a deeper truth, one that transcends the movie: *you're not the only person who hurts.* There are no coincidences in life. By accessing something bigger than ourselves, we discover we can change our future and live a life we want to live.

"I can change the way I feel." Sometimes we initiate change in our lives, and sometimes change comes to us and changes everything. Our thoughts come and go. However, our beliefs, actions, and desires are attached to our thoughts, and those form the basis of our reality. When we understand we can influence our thoughts, and the thoughts of others, in a positive rather than a negative direction, this is the beginning of understanding our abilities and responsibilities as everyday coaches. There's never only one chance, and there's always time for redemption, both as an individual and as an everyday coach.

—What is your "raining frogs" moment?

—How are your thoughts, beliefs, actions, and desires influencing your reality?

CHAPTER 5

FAILURE'S GIFT

Failure can take many different forms: failure on the field, personal and professional failure, and failing to be an effective everyday coach. But failure isn't the last word. Failure is actually a gift. It's a miss that can be attempted a different way next time, moving us forward and allowing us to improve our skills, redirect our steps, and refocus our efforts. We can learn to take the punch in the face and stay engaged.

"Everybody thinks they can fight till they get hit in the face." General Uberti says,

> There's a quote that says, "Everybody's a good boxer till they get hit in the face." At West Point, every cadet boxes. There's always somebody faster, stronger, and better. The goal is to instill readiness, to help people realize they can take a punch and get back up. Boxing teaches us to take a punch and stay engaged. In life, we're going to get hit. Sometimes it will hurt more than other times. Despite that, we can recognize we all have an obligation to help those around us. It's about putting others first.

Cedric King says it this way: "This [losing my legs] is the greatest gift, because it taught me how to be a better me. Who we really are is not what we do. Don't confuse what you do with who you are. What you do is your role. Who you are is your identity. We find out who we are in the trenches. And who we are doesn't change depending on our uniform."

Deposits in our resiliency account. My dad once told me, "Harrison, at some point in life, everyone gets a royal f*#%@. The sooner it happens to you, the luckier you are." What does that mean? Some life experiences, like divorce, a serious medical diagnosis, job loss, and unanticipated events and changes, are inevitable. They happen in the course of life itself. In everyday coaching, that "sooner and luckier" statement means allowing people to fully experience the course that's set for them.

Some things we can control, and some things we can't. As excruciating as it is to watch from the sidelines, despite our own knowledge, perspective, fears, and desire to protect our people from that "royal f*#%@," we have to let the situation take its natural course. It's such a hard thing as parents and coaches who would rather protect our people from negative consequences caused by things that aren't their fault, but we cannot spare our people the valuable life lessons that come from these experiences. Consider these lessons deposits in our "resiliency account." Protecting our people from the negative consequences of their own choices and actions as well as those of others just delays the consequences until the stakes are much higher.

What does overprotective look like?

- Comforting a child quickly after a simple fall that produces no distress

- Strict rules that do not allow a child to get dirty or be creative

- Punishment that does not fit the crime; overly harsh discipline for minor offenses

- Over-emphasis on academic success

- Heavy reliance on a system of rewards and punishments

- Doing our child's homework, even just a little

- Talking to adults for them

- Blaming others for the child's inadequacies, delinquencies, and shortcomings[9]

The consequence of overprotective relationships might not show up for years or decades, but emphasizing unquestioning compliance over open communication eventually takes a relational toll. Protecting our people, whether they're our children, colleagues, or athletes, from the anticipation of bad experiences, hurt feelings, rejection, and failure can keep them from developing the skills essential to coping with life experiences.[10] When that "royal f*#%@" comes, and it will, they will be under-equipped to deal with it effectively.

What is our end goal? Are we trying to make life easy in the short run, or coach them to be resourceful, effective, successful adults?

Protecting our people from the negative consequences of their own choices and actions as well as those of others just delays the consequences until the stakes are much higher.

The opponent inside of us. As everyday coaches, we want what's best for our people. We want to see them happy and successful, thinking independently and able to self-regulate their emotions, actions, and reactions.[11] This is especially true when we're parenting our kids. According to leadership expert Tim Elmore, "When we rescue too quickly and overindulge our children with 'assistance,' we remove the need for them to navigate hardships and solve problems on their own. This prohibits them from becoming competent adults."[12]

Instead of always coming to others' rescue, Cedric King suggests this: letting our people fail, or fall, and recover, and then encouraging them to come back and try again. What if we say to them, "You go figure it out," and actually let them do that? "If the hardest thing we face in our life is a barista who messes up our coffee order, what happens when we face really hard stuff?" he asks. "Do the things you know you need to do. Be proud of what you do and who you are. Do hard stuff every day. Overcome the opponent that's inside of you. To be a great leader of people, you've got to be a great leader of *you.*"

CHAPTER 6

ENCOURAGING FAILURE

Maryland's Winningest Coach. 221 wins. 14 conference championships. 29 years of coaching football. 10 trips to the NCAA playoffs. 2018 Division III Coach of the Year. Johns Hopkins University Head Coach Jim Margraff was the winningest football coach in Johns Hopkins history and Maryland state history. He was a man who knew what he was about and who made the most not just of his time, but the time of those around him. It was about more than football with him. He wasn't old in years, but he lived a full life. His lasting influence will carry that life forward. He figured it out. He wrote his own definition of success. And he lived out what he knew best and believed most: *You can be competitive and still be content.*

Margraff-isms:
"Don't spend your time, invest your time."
"Pressure is for surgeons and soldiers, not football players."
"Carry yourself with pride and poise."
"Your reputation is like a redwood tree. It takes many years to grow, but it only takes 15 minutes to cut down."
"Two things you can never get back: a spent arrow and a spoken word."

Trust isn't needed in predictable situations, when everyone knows what to expect. But when stakes are high and outcomes are unclear, trust is the bridge between where we are and where we're going.

A bridge of trust. "When you have a bedrock of trust between you as coach and your people, you believe in each other," says Martin Rooney, founder and head coach, Training for Warriors. Rooney is an internationally recognized coach, fitness expert, bestselling author and pioneer of strength and conditioning; former COO of the Parisi Speed School; and member of the 1996 United States Olympic Bobsled Team. "Your people know you're going to love them whether they succeed or not. There is so much pressure to succeed, and yet success doesn't depend on their performance on the field.

"Let your people know that in the scheme of the universe, their best effort is enough. Don't let fear of failure keep us from giving our best effort."

Coach Margraff understood the necessity and the essence of establishing and maintaining trust among his people. How did he do it so effectively, and what can we take away from his "everyday coach" approach?

1. By communicating and enforcing expectations

2. By holding everyone accountable to the same standard

Our people need to know what to expect when things go the way we want them to, and when they don't, and they need to trust that we'll have their backs when things don't go as expected.

"People are going to make mistakes, so give them permission to make mistakes and keep coming back until they get it," says Cedric King. "We need to believe in our people beyond their failures. Believe in them not because they *are* good, but because they *can be* good. So we make mistakes. Our mistakes aren't who we are!

NFL head coach Ron Rivera once told me, "I'm not in the football business. I'm in the business of making good men. Men who say, 'I'm going to play through contact until I hear the whistle.'" Things happen in life, and we still have to make a way and not wait for a pass.

When Coach Rivera was fired from his position, he said, "I'm so thankful for this organization. They gave me a chance." He reframed the situation by understanding it was time to move on to the next thing and find an opportunity to succeed somewhere else.

"We need everyday coaches," King concludes. "Because none of us can do this alone. Somebody has to help us push through our perceived limits and see that 'better' is already inside us."

CHAPTER 7

OVERCOMING THE FEAR OF FAILURE

Give it our best effort. It takes courage to miss, and to strike out. Whether we're a highly trained Olympic athlete or a gangly middle school kid in our first track and field meet, every time we compete in the high jump or pole vault, it must end in failure. The goal is to miss three times in these events. Otherwise, the officials keep raising the bar, and we get the opportunity to get our misses up.

We always have a choice. We always have a choice: we can choose to be afraid, or we can choose to move forward through and beyond our fear. In her memoir *The Choice: Embrace the Possible,* Holocaust survivor Dr. Edith Eva Eger says, "This is the work of healing. You deny what hurts, what you fear. You avoid it at all costs. Then you find a way to welcome and embrace what you're most afraid of. And then you can finally let it go."[13]

As everyday coaches, what can we do to help people overcome their fear of failure?

- Think rationally about potential outcomes, from best-case to worst-case scenario. What's the worst thing that can happen? What's the best thing that can happen?

- Remember that everything is recoverable and the future holds endless possibilities for future successes, even in the very next moment.

- Set precise, reachable goals to build confidence that gradually increases over time. Focus on doing the next right thing.

- Develop contingency plans for times when things don't go the way we expect or hope they will.

- Replace negative self-talk with a narrative of affirmation always.

- Focus on what we can do. Imagine how it will feel.[14]

Helping People Overcome Fear of Failure

Coaching and playing to grow. The hallmark of the most successful everyday coaches isn't 100% success all the time. It's a desire to learn, and to translate that knowledge into success on the field. "How often do we see assistant coaches and instructors step into roles of more responsibility after being mentored by successful coaches?" asks Gregg Williams, who has more than 30 years of experience as an NFL head coach and defensive coordinator. "Success isn't measured only by wins and losses. It's 'Are you learning? Are you growing?' It's not only about playing to win or lose. It's about playing to grow. It's about discovering the limits of how good we can be and continuing to push those limits. Eventually, we become so comfortable in the zone of taking risks that failure no longer intimidates us."

—How can we exemplify a higher standard?

—How can we take risks and encourage others to do the same in the face of anticipated failure?

"The finish line is a myth," says Cedric King. "There's always something to wake up to and do better. It's a lifestyle, not a destination. 'Better' is always better than 'best.' Our ongoing challenge is to be better tomorrow than we were today. There ain't no finish line!"

Remember: the secret to successful, lasting results is *not quitting. Not* not failing...*not quitting.*

After-Action Review

•There's a difference between fearing failure and fearing the feeling of failure.

•Giving fear less power results in 'fear less.'

•We can choose to change the way we feel.

•We can overcome the opponent inside us.

•Failure brings us the opportunity to push through perceived limits.

•'Better' is better than 'best' when we're playing and coaching to grow.

•Good or bad, we have a lasting impact as everyday coaches.

PART 2
COMPEL

– Redefining our "why"

CHAPTER 8

"THIS IS YOUR TIME"

In the 1980 Lake Placid Olympics, moments before the USA National Hockey Team faced off against the Soviet Union National Hockey Team, Coach Herb Brooks spoke to his players.

> *Great moments are born from great opportunity. And that's what you have here tonight, boys. That's what you've earned here tonight. One game. If we played 'em ten times, they might win nine. But not this game. Not tonight. Tonight, we skate with them. Tonight, we stay with them. And we shut them down because we can! Tonight, WE are the greatest hockey team in the world. You were born to be hockey players. Every one of you. And you were meant to be here tonight. This is your time. Their time is done. It's over. I'm sick and tired of hearing about what a great hockey team the Soviets have. Screw 'em. This is your time. Now go out there and take it.*

The Soviets held five Olympic gold medals, 16 world titles, and 19 European championships. Most played professional hockey, and six of them were playing in their third Olympics. Their goaltender, Vladislav Tretiak, was considered the best in hockey.

By contrast, the American team, the youngest in national team history, was primarily amateur players. Their coach, Herb Brooks, pushed them beyond what they thought was possible. "He questioned their pride," says an article from the *Seattle Times*. "He pushed, prodded, insulted. They questioned his militaristic approach. He wasn't always popular with them. They even nicknamed Brooks' merciless wind sprints, from red line to red line and back again, 'Herbies.'"[15]

The USA pulled ahead with 10 minutes left in the third period. In an impossibly tense battle on ice, they won the game 4-3, and the victory is still considered one of the most iconic in American sports history. After beating Finland in the final match-up, they earned the Olympic gold medal.

(On a side note, contrast this with Herb Brooks's speech before the gold medal-determining game against Finland: coming into the dressing room for the second intermission, Brooks turned to his players, looked at them, and said, "If you lose this game, you'll take it to your f*#%@ graves." He then walked towards the locker room door, paused, looked over his shoulder, and said to them again, "Your f*#%@ graves.")[16]

One more thing of note: in their last exhibition game on February 9, 1980, the Soviet team defeated the American team 10-3. This victory caused the Soviets to greatly underestimate the American team in their next matchup on February 22.

* * * * *

CHAPTER 9

THE BRAIDED ROPE OF INSPIRATION AND MOTIVATION

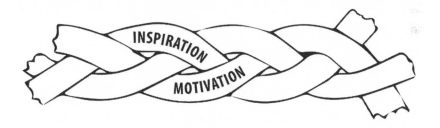

Inspiration and motivation are closely intertwined, almost like a braided rope. General Casey says, "Inspiration (the commitment to excellence) is a group mindset. Motivation is the individual determination to go the extra mile to prepare to contribute to the success of the team."

A collection of motivated individuals makes an inspired team. A collection of inspired individuals creates a motivated team. And an inspired, motivated team having fun has an unrivaled competitive edge.

CHAPTER 10

THE SECRET TO INFLUENCING OTHERS

Everyday coaching is influencing others to do something we want them to do because they want to do it. Notice the word 'influence.' It's not forcing, manipulating, demanding, or threatening. Influencing is helping others achieve more than they imagine or see for themselves. Former President Dwight Eisenhower defined it this way: "Leadership is the art of getting someone else to do something you want done because they want to do it."

"Leadership is the art of getting someone else to do something you want done because they want to do it." – President Dwight D. Eisenhower

* * * * *

What is influencing and how do we do it? Do we ever catch ourselves asking, even in our own minds, *"Why can't I get people to behave the way I want them to? Kids, boss, employees, teammates, spouse… If they would just (fill in the blank), then I could (fill in the blank)."*

We can't force people to be different than they are, but we can influence situations by giving people the autonomy to be themselves while behaving in a way that's within the boundaries for the outcome we hope to achieve. By influencing environment (context and surroundings) and expectations, we influence behavior.

This is true leadership: influencing people to do what **we** want them to do because **they** want to do it. This is the essence of everyday coaching. Successful everyday coaching is an ongoing journey to understanding why and how we inspire, motivate, and influence the people we relate to and interact with every day.

By influencing environment and expectations, we influence behavior.

* * * * *

CHAPTER 11

THE AMAZING POWER OF OUR MIND

During the winter off-season of 2007, I joined my fellow Washington Redskins football team strength coaches on a tour of the best sports performance programs in the country. One of our stops was the US Olympic Training Facility in Colorado Springs.

I was excited to see the USA Olympic weightlifting practice and found myself standing in their gym. This gym looks nothing like a health club or CrossFit box. It is an enormous square with vaulted ceilings and weightlifting platforms neatly organized in a grid. There are stackable boxes, weightlifting racks which are merely two posts standing vertically with a little J-hook at the top to rest a bar, and bumper plates and weights lined up beside each platform. There are also two folding metal chairs per platform and chalk buckets. There is no other equipment in this room. It's just you and gravity staring at each other eye to eye, preparing for a 90-minute battle.

The other remarkable detail about this room is its absolute silence. No one talks. If, and only if, something needs to be verbally communicated between a coach and a lifter, it is an inaudible whisper. The only sound you can actually hear is the zing of the bar on lift-off, the crack of wood-heeled weightlifting shoes smashing the floor, the gentle sing of the weights at the top of an attempt, and the thud of the bar as gravity returns it to the platform. The entire purpose of this environment is to promote intense focus.

I marveled at a 140 lb. female Olympic lifter who just pushed 240 lbs. over her head twice as a work set. Then I noticed a male lifter sitting on the floor with headphones on, eyes shut, head down, sweating profusely. "Is this guy sick?" I wondered. "Should we get help? Why is everyone ignoring him?" Come to find out, that guy was actually lifting… *in his mind.*

He was able to focus so intensely and visualize his entire training program that he actually created a physiological response in his body. I watched him sweat through his clothes and his breathing change as he virtually attempted each lift in his brain. When the team was done working out, he left the gym just as exhausted as everyone else. And the wildest part was, he literally got stronger!

An interesting fact we know from neuroscience is that the regions of the brain that activate when we imagine a movement using mental imagery are the same regions that activate when we actually perform the same movement.

One popular study, entitled "From mental power to muscle power—gaining strength by using the mind," found that participants who completed mental contractions without physical training in abduction of their little finger and elbow flexion over 12 weeks had significant strength gains compared to a control group who did zero training, either mental or physical. The eight participants who were training their little finger abduction strength gained 35% percent strength improvement. The elbow flexion group gained 13.5% strength gains over a 12-week period. The results of this study prove we can get physically stronger by imagining getting stronger![17]

Descartes' Error and the body loop. Dr. Antonio Damasio, a famous neuroscientist, came up with something called the Somatic Marker Hypothesis described in his book, *Descartes' Error.* This hypothesis states that our decisions are influenced by somatic markers, physical sensations like rapid heartbeat or stomach cramps. These somatic markers (physical sensations) are associated with our emotions. "When we are afraid of something," says Dr. Damasio, "our hearts begin to race, our mouths become dry, our skin turns pale and our muscles contract. This emotional reaction occurs automatically and unconsciously. Feelings occur after we become aware in our brain of such physical changes; only then do we experience the feeling of fear."[18]

In addition, our emotions are associated with past events and potential future outcomes. Think about how you might feel just prior to giving a public speech in front of one thousand people. Maybe you have an elevated heart rate and feel nervous. The stronger these somatic markers are when stimulated in these situations, the stronger our emotional association becomes, which influences our thoughts and decisions. Dr. Damasio calls this the "body loop."

The "as-if" body loop. We also know from neuroscience that our thoughts (which are imagined) actually rewire our brain, which changes our interpretation of these somatic markers and their accompanied emotions. The contrived emotional response influences our somatic markers, which further changes our emotions and then influences our decisions. Dr. Damasio calls this the "as-if body loop."

Body loops in action. Imagine you are a football coach making a decision to either earn a first down on 4th & 3 or punt. Once you make this decision, you must decide on the play you want to call and who you want to execute the play. Time is ticking, and the outcome of the game is on the line. Good health will prevent hypertension from poor diet and exercise from accelerating your heart rate, which is subconsciously influencing your emotions and your decisions. It will also help to be spiritually and psychologically fit, so that you know how to properly regulate your somatic and emotional response. We'll explore this more in depth later.

Now imagine you are in a supermarket and your two-year-old is throwing a tantrum. This is your only opportunity to do your grocery shopping for the week, and your spouse is counting on you to get it done. You're facing a series of critical decisions at this moment: since you're being observed by fellow shoppers, your public reputation is on the line, your actions will impact your young child, and you're accountable to your household for buying needed food. This is when you need to be the most physically, mentally, and spiritually fit to make the best everyday coaching decision. Do you make a decision based on your perception of others' opinions, on the conflict between what you need to do (shop for food) and what circumstances are dictating (toddler in full blown tantrum mode), and on how are you influenced by your own emotional responses? Are you able to objectively evaluate options in the stress of that moment? How beneficial would it be to consider possible outcomes and solutions to this situation in your mind before you're in that moment?

In retrospect, apart from our "body loop" of somatic markers, we'll know exactly what the best decision would have been at the time. "I could have," or "I should have...," or "I wish I would have..." is a common response. Our goal as everyday coaches is to learn to evaluate options objectively, training ourselves to make the best decisions before the situations arise.

CHAPTER 12

OUR INSPIRATIONAL 'WHY'

The Spark of Inspiration. Have you ever heard or said about a player or team, "They're playing inspired ball!" Sometimes, in the wake of an event or a tragedy that affects an entire team or organization, a team takes the field knowing they're representing something or someone much larger than themselves. Their effort is fueled by their desire to remember or honor that person or event and their desire to win. They're playing inspired ball.

On Nov. 14, 1970, a chartered jet carrying a five-member flight crew, 36 Marshall University (WV) football players, five coaches, the athletic director, four other members of the athletic department and 24 fans crashed into a hillside while returning from a game at East Carolina. There were no survivors. It was the worst sports-related disaster in American history. Despite the overwhelming loss, the university's acting president announced the school's football program would continue. The following year, with a new coach, the team was given special permission from the NCAA to play freshmen. With very few experienced players, the team won two of its 10 games that year, including an upset win over Xavier on the last play of the game. The 1970 and 1971 teams "laid the groundwork" for Marshall's future football successes, according to assistant coach Red Dawson.

Those successes include 20 consecutive winning seasons, two of them undefeated; eight conference crowns; two I-AA national championships; five bowl wins; and multiple players who went on to the NFL. Marshall finished the 1990s with 114 victories, more than any other team in I-A or I-AA in a single decade.[19]

Obviously we don't want our athletes constantly reeling from devastating personal tragedy in order to play their best game, or our people constantly functioning in a state of shock and grief. Short of that, is there a way we can compel them to perform at the level of "inspired" all the time? On the ball field, in the office, or at home, the most important thing is to inspire our people. When that inspiration catches fire, it carries the whole team forward.

What drives the fire. Imagine we're building a fire. The inspiration for the fire is to generate heat and produce energy. Inspiration isn't the fuel. It's not the spark. It's the reason the fire exists in the first place. With heat and energy, we can change an object into something completely different. The need for the fire and its purpose becomes our inspirational WHY. It's our emotional drive to do what we do, a force that propels us forward and makes things happen.

Our inspirational WHY is the purpose, cause, or belief that drives every organization and every person's individual career or performance. It's the flame that sustains the heat and energy. It influences our identity, individually and as a group. Best-selling author, speaker, and optimist Simon Sinek says, "If we want to feel an undying passion for our work, if we want to feel we are contributing to something bigger than ourselves, we all need to know our WHY."[20]

"Discovering the WHY injects passion into our work,"[21] says Sinek. Inspiration speaks to a feeling of alliance with something bigger. Establishing a compelling inspirational "why" takes time and deep reflection.

For instance, the concept of "selfless selfishness" draws from the guiding principle behind morality, often referred to as the Golden Rule: love your neighbor as yourself. Not "more than yourself" or "less than yourself," but "as yourself." While selfishness can be perceived as both good and bad, selflessness is not possible without first being selfish: taking care of ourselves. Taking care of ourselves helps us care for those around us more effectively. More importantly, taking care of others helps us become better people, and often contributes to discovering our "why."

Our "why" tells the story of our "what," and our "how." According to Sinek, what we do serves as the proof of what we believe. And our *why* shapes our *what*. Establishing our "why" is at the core of everything that flows out from that inspiration, and a clear "why" grounds our truth – our authenticity.

CHAPTER 13

INTENTIONAL INSPIRATION

Soldiers To Sidelines believes so strongly in the importance and role of inspiration in everyday coaching that we have developed a three-step process to help achieve it.

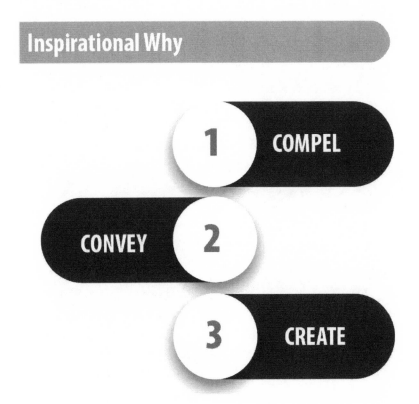

Inspirational Why

1 COMPEL

CONVEY 2

3 CREATE

This can be deceptively difficult. However, every story of successful inspiration, including the story of the improbable 1980 United States Olympic hockey team victory, seems to follow this pattern or structure.

Building commitment by demonstrating it ourselves. *Inspiration* speaks to internal incentives: speaking into a desire to do and be better, to have more self-respect, to make others proud, things that are longer term and less quantifiable. It's a harder place to get to because of its amorphous, ethereal, longer-lasting, deeper meaning and nature. What intangible feelings do we associate with inspiration? If we know those, we can coach to them.

Servant-based leadership is the essence of everyday coaching. Are we willing to commit all our energy and resources to make a person, team, and organization better without receiving any recognition whatsoever, knowing we will never be able to claim or receive credit for any of the success? This is the essence of servant-based leadership.

Over the past 20 years coaching in strength and conditioning and in football, I have watched many private coaches develop flourishing businesses as the next guru in a specific aspect of sport. Among other things, they specialize in speed training, pitching, quarterback technique, defensive back school, hitting coach, serve coach, and forehand guru. At one point I was one of them.

What always concerned me was that many of the coaches who had tremendous ability began staking their claim on the athlete's success. "I trained Kevin Durant, I developed Brian Cushing, I discovered Mike Trout, etc." This claim seemed absurd to me, because a coach is such a small, albeit powerful, influence in an athlete's life. The athlete's success is predicated on dozens of people's assistance throughout their life, most importantly their parents and peers.

If a baseball player is able to ascend to the professional level of playing for the New York Yankees, he most likely had several coaches. For instance, MLB catcher Austin Romine, who at the time this book was written (2020) played for the Detroit Tigers, had about 17 baseball coaches from high school until he made the New York Yankees roster in 2011. His dad played for the Boston Red Sox. How many times did he work out with a personal trainer or a private hitting coach? Who on that list could actually claim they alone developed him into a baseball star?

A common goal and a commitment to excellence. "You build a team around a common goal," General Casey says. "That's your compelling "why." You're washing the individual out of the equation. It's all about commitment to something larger than themselves."

> Excellence is about getting people to commit to something they don't think they can do. People want to be excellent, but the vast majority don't have the discipline and drive to do it by themselves. However, they can do it as part of a team. To me, inspiration starts with a common goal and a commitment to excellence.
>
> As a lieutenant in the Army, I was assigned to my first platoon in Germany, preparing for a big inspection in which they inspected every piece of equipment in the entire platoon, including each individual. I determined we would be the best. This required hard work and late hours and involved a lot of grousing. "You're not the other guys," I growled. "You're better than them." At the end of the inspection, I was told, "Lieutenant, of all the platoons I've seen, this one is far and away the best." The guys had left their positions where they were standing at attention and had gathered around just outside the door to hear the results. When they heard those words, they erupted in cheers. It wasn't about me, it was about them committing to succeed as a group. When they worked hard as individuals, they succeeded as a group. I

was there with them the whole time; I didn't ask them to do anything I wasn't prepared to do myself.

Inspiration and motivation are the starting points in building a good team. It separates the great teams from the good teams, and great everyday coaches from all the other coaches.

CHAPTER 14

ESTABLISHING STANDARDS AND HOLDING PEOPLE ACCOUNTABLE

According to General Casey, inspiration and motivation consist of establishing standards and holding people accountable.

"When you set standards, you have to be clear about what you want people to do," he explains.

> As for accountability and reward, if you meet the standard, there's a reward; if you don't, there's a sanction. It's as simple as "that's not the route we want you to run; take a lap." Napoleon figured out that men would die for a ribbon or a medal. Reward what you value, and hold people accountable when they don't meet the standard.
>
> Disciplined adherence to exacting standards brings people to excellence. Everybody wants to do something once and think they've got it. As a Lieutenant Colonel, my goal was to win at the National Training Center, our version of the Super Bowl. The opposing team lived there and played there all the time. They were the best of the best. They had the home field advantage. If you were going to be the best, you had to beat these guys.
>
> What did we have to be really good at? Tactics, physical fitness, maintenance, and logistics. I established a Commander's Award for excellence in all those areas. We established standards for everything

so everyone knew what was expected. Every unit competed for those standards. They weren't competing against each other; they were competing against the standards.

CHAPTER 15

MOTIVATION

If inspiration is establishing our compelling "why," then motivation is the day-to-day promotion of that initial inspiration. It's consistently taking the action needed to pursue our "why."

Motivation

What is Motivation?

A — The reason or reasons we have for acting or behaving in a particular way

B — Influencing our people to do what they might not enjoy now in order to achieve something they love in the future

C — Do what we should over what we want

Motivation can be both positive and negative. We're motivated by economic incentives, fear, and reward. We can generate short-term behavior changes in ourselves and our people if we dangle specific rewards: do something challenging at a certain level or for a certain time, and receive this reward in return. However, by itself, it can be a temporary short-term effect and can even have a negative effect afterward because of the need for constantly generating new, bigger, and better incentives. It's not the best way to build long-term commitment in ourselves and our people.

CHAPTER 16

THE SPECTRUM OF INFLUENCE

Unsuccessful motivation. Unsuccessful motivation still exerts force and generates action. That action may take the form of skepticism, resistance, or outright rebellion. Consider the motivation of financial gain, either nominal or substantial. Instead of being a successful motivator, financial gain may actually be an unsuccessful motivator.

For instance, years ago, in an attempt to control the population of venomous cobras plaguing the citizens of Delhi, India, the British Colonial government offered a financial bounty for every dead cobra brought to the administration officials. Initially, the plan seemed successful. Snake catchers claimed their bounties and fewer cobras were seen in the city. But instead of tapering off over time, there was a steady increase in the number of dead cobras being presented for bounty payment each month. Why?

Under the new policy, cobra bounties provided a stable source of income. In addition, it was much easier to kill captive cobras than to hunt them in the city. So the snake catchers increasingly abandoned their search for wild cobras, and concentrated on breeding programs. In time, the government, puzzled by the discrepancy between the number of cobras seen around the city and the number of dead cobras redeemed for bounty payments, discovered the clandestine breeding sites, and abandoned the bounty policy. As a final act the breeders, now stuck with nests of worthless cobras, simply released them into the city, making the problem even worse than before.[22]

* * * * *

In a similar instance, American financial institution Wells Fargo seemed to be beating the odds in a bad economy. During the financial crisis in 2008, the bank acquired Wachovia to become the third-largest bank by assets in the United States. A few years later, its growing revenue and soaring stock brought the company's value to nearly $300 billion. But behind this success was a company culture that drove employees to open fraudulent accounts in an attempt to reach lofty sales goals. Between 2011 and 2015, company employees opened more than 1.5 million bank accounts and applied for over 565,000 credit cards that may not have been authorized.

Many former employees reported that company sales goals were impossible to meet, and incentives for compensation and ongoing employment encouraged gaming the system. One former employee described it as a "grind-house," with co-workers "cracking under pressure." Another former employee reported, "If you don't meet your solutions you're not a team player. If you're bringing down the team then you will be fired and it will be on your permanent record."[23]

* * * * *

Other types of unsuccessful motivation include demanding, which results in limited, grudging compliance, yelling, which causes our people to tune out and resent the negative influence, and, like we saw in the two instances above, exchange, which generates an immediate result with the long-term potential for negative effects. These actions may exert force and generate action, but they don't necessarily move our people in a desired direction.

INFLUENCE SPECTRUM

After Terry Bacon, *Elements of Influence*

What do we want and how do we get there? Let's take a look at the other side of the influence spectrum.

CHAPTER 17

OUR MOTIVATIONAL "WHY"

Successful motivation spurs the sacrifices we make individually and as a team or group to achieve excellence. It convinces us to do something we may not want to do so we can achieve a desired result. When our "should do" and our "want to do" become the same, our inspiration and motivation join forces and we position ourselves and our people to succeed.

When our "should do" and our "want to do" become the same, our inspiration and motivation join forces and we position ourselves and our people to succeed.

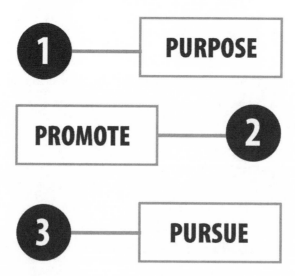

Motivational Why

1 — PURPOSE

PROMOTE — 2

3 — PURSUE

Three steps of motivation:

1 - **Purposing our motivational "why"** - Our "why" is our purpose or reason for acting or behaving a certain way. Motivation begins by establishing and clearly stating our "why." That initial step is a necessary precursor to the next two steps of motivation.

Simon Sinek defines our "why" as "the purpose, cause, or belief that drives every one of us." We can describe what we do, and often explain how we do it. But it's harder to articulate the "why" behind the "what" and the "how."

Our "why" springs from a sense that we're aligned with something bigger than just ourselves. There's a "why" behind the writing of this book. Our "why" is more than just what we know, think, or do. How we feel about something or someone is more powerful than what we think about it or them.[24] Our feelings and our thoughts, when combined, generate emotional alignment. That, in turn, influences our loyalty to certain teams, breeds, brands, and ways of doing things. It's a way of identifying what's most important to us, lining our choices and behaviors up to carry that identification forward, connecting with other people who share that same sense of emotional alignment, and accomplishing more together than we ever imagined on our own.

Where inspiration can be all over the place, wild and exciting, motivation is much more focused. When we feel inspiration for something, no matter what it is, our passion can change at the whim of our own emotions and our feelings.

Motivation, on the other hand, keeps us going when results don't turn out the way we expect or when we're criticized by others. Motivation isn't tied to single, or even multiple, attempts to achieve a goal. It's focused on the big picture. When we find our motivational "why," we focus on the one thing that will satisfy and complete us. Inspiration will ebb and flow, but motivation endures. We can achieve one goal and work toward another one. Motivation weaves throughout our lives for the long term.

"Passion *[what we call inspiration]* focuses on nouns. What do you love? It's about the objects of your desires. Purpose is your motivation, your why. It brings in action so it focuses on verbs. Purpose *[motivation]* completes you," says entrepreneur George Krueger.[25]

Try this exercise: Establishing our why. To *(action)* so that *(result)*. What action is important to you, and what does doing that make possible?

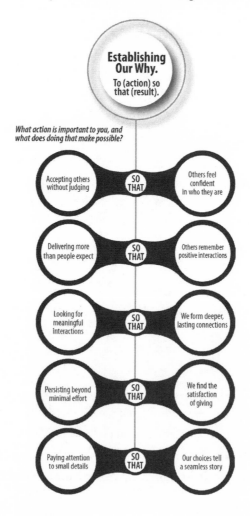

2 - Promoting our "why" – Once we establish our "why," we need to promote it. Some ways to do this:

Promoting Our Why

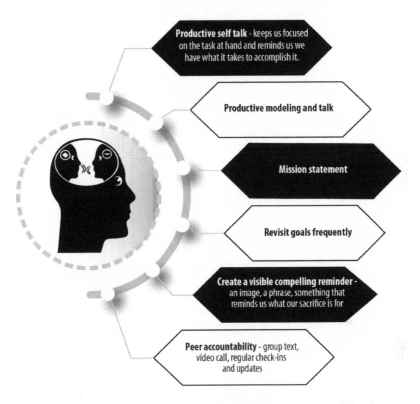

- **Productive self talk** - keeps us focused on the task at hand and reminds us we have what it takes to accomplish it.
- **Productive modeling and talk**
- **Mission statement**
- **Revisit goals frequently**
- **Create a visible compelling reminder** - an image, a phrase, something that reminds us what our sacrifice is for
- **Peer accountability** - group text, video call, regular check-ins and updates

It's been said that most people quit when they're just 10% of the distance from the finish line. Even when we can't see how close we are to finishing, we can continually promote our purpose to ourselves and our people. As everyday coaches, our job is to keep that end goal constantly in view so our people don't give up when they're 90% there.

There's even a tongue-in-cheek rule called the 90/90 rule. Bell Labs' Tom Cargill, a world-renowned computer programming expert, is widely credited with saying, "The first 90 percent of the code accounts for the first 90 percent of the development time. The remaining 10 percent of the code accounts for the other 90 percent of the development time."

3 - Pursuing our "why" – Establishing and remembering our "why" creates the foundation for the essential third step: pursuing our "why." In order to do that, we need to understand that there is a spectrum for motivation. At its core, motivation either pushes us or pulls us, depending on whether we're motivated by fear or encouragement. Successful motivation moves us from apathy (not caring one way or another) to compliance, commitment, and eventual leadership.

Visualizing what we're working toward. When I worked with the Washington Redskins football team, every day when we came to work, the first thing we encountered when we entered the building was a huge glass case containing three Super Bowl trophies. Everyone who worked for the organization passed those trophies every day, often many times a day. It was a prominent reminder of why we came to work every day and what we were working toward. Without a single word, those trophies said, "This is what we're trying to achieve. This is what we're investing ourselves in. This isn't just our past; it's our future."

In the movie *Miracle*, referenced earlier, about the 1980 U.S. Olympic hockey team's victory over the Soviet Union, in the U.S. locker room, an entire wall was covered with telegrams wishing the team luck. Every time anyone entered and left that space, they passed those telegrams. It was a compelling visual reminder of their purpose – what they were there to achieve, and why it mattered so much.

—*What visual reminders can we display to motivate ourselves and our people?*

—*Is there a way to create a vision of motivation to remind ourselves, and our people, "This is what we're trying to achieve?"*

CHAPTER 18

MOTIVATION IN ACTION - "PURPLE FINGER DAY"

As for motivating people when they think they can't do something, General Casey recalls,

> So much about leadership has to do with the conviction or vision of the coach or leader. Establishing a vision means making judgments about the future. It requires the courage to make choices and to act. For instance, we had five months to prepare for the first elections in Iraq that would elect a government to write the Iraqi constitution. The elections would be held at the end of January 2005. We put together a plan. I wasn't sure it would work, but I had conviction and drove it into the organization. They started to believe, and a couple of successful battles gave us confidence.
>
> When the Iraqis voted, they dipped their right index finger in indelible purple ink to prove they'd voted. The news showed people walking around staring at their purple fingers, amazed at the proof they'd participated in the election. [Secretary of Defense] Donald Rumsfeld called me and said, "When the eyes of the world were upon you, you stood and delivered." Having the conviction, and having a reasonable plan, and encouraging people to infuse them with confidence, and having interim successes along the way, all made this work.
>
> You don't start out winning the Super Bowl. But you generate momentum toward your inspiration by stringing together a series of

successes, things you reach for that are a stretch but everybody comes together and accomplishes them. That accomplishment gives them confidence in themselves and in their leader.

To accomplish the successful elections, we had to do two major things: 1 – Reduce the safe havens, parts of the country controlled by terrorists and insurgents, and 2 – strengthen Iraqi security forces so they could secure their own polling sites. We went through a series of operations where we cleaned out the safe havens. Every time we did that successfully, that moved us one step closer to where we were going. There was a terribly difficult battle in Fallujah, the last major stronghold, and we succeeded in about 10 days and that took the wind out of the bad guys and opened the door for successful elections. Meanwhile, we were measuring the Iraqi security forces, and how many are capable of guarding polling sites, and those numbers grew over time.

Every time we met a goal, I publicized the hell out of it. We said we were going to do this, and we did it. We were on track. Part of motivation is that people need to see how what they're doing in the bowels of the organization contributes to the larger whole. I couldn't tell people enough about how what they were doing contributed. People need to see how their efforts contribute to major success.

There are reasons, and there are DEEP REASONS. Deep reasons generate understanding. They show people what they're doing right and create opportunities for success, which far exceeds just not making a mistake. The purple finger represented success. When they started seeing people on television walking around with purple fingers, more Iraqi people went out to vote. It was a powerful visible reminder of success.

The story related by General Casey perfectly illustrates motivation – his people established, promoted, and pursued their purpose. They invested their best effort in the potential to create better lives for the people they were serving. Their resulting success still resonates today.

Setting and reaching goals. As evidenced by the braided rope illustration in Chapter 9, we need BOTH inspiration and motivation. We can motivate by firing people up and reliving past experiences. We can inspire by setting the example, being the role model, mentoring, coaching, and encouraging others. Inspiring and motivating others helps us understand them. Jack Talley, general manager and vice president of Enterprise Rent-A-Car's southwest group, says, "Good leaders know the lessons their people are learning are life lessons. Think about the importance of saying, hearing, and believing, 'There's good in everybody.' 'Every day is good. Some days are better.' 'Others have it worse than us.' 'Was that your best effort?' and 'Your best is good enough.'" As everyday coaches, we can choose what to coach and when by not allowing bad behavior, and coaching to the good behavior we want repeated.

"I don't have a set strategy to inspire people," says Bill MacDonald, Founding Partner, CEO, President, and Chief Investment Officer, Mill Creek Residential. "Whatever I preach, I also do. I'm committed to setting the right example and to being available. I don't micromanage, but I do encourage."

Bill describes his process for setting and reaching goals this way:

1. Set goals – where do we want to be, what do we want to look like?

2. Where are we today?

3. Map out what gets us from here to there – here's what we need to do

For example, when envisioning recapitalizing a company, the process might look like this:

1. Here's what we have and where we are today.

2. Here's what double that looks like.

3. How do we get there in five years?

Our motivational "why" ties into our ultimate goal and helps us visualize the journey to get there.

CHAPTER 19

THE LIFELONG PRACTICE OF EVERYDAY COACHING

Practice isn't just for those we coach. The practice of coaching is similar to the practice of law or medicine. It's an ongoing process. There are rules and fundamentals, but as everyday coaches, if our goal is to inspire a lifelong love of learning in our people, we need to set the example and be continually learning the art of everyday coaching ourselves. There's always something we can learn and put into practice in our lives as well as the lives of those we're coaching. Practicing isn't just for our people!

We are coaches in every aspect of our life, every single day, and we don't even realize it. We are always influencing and developing the people around us.

Woven together, both inspiration and motivation make the rope stronger. Both are essential in our lives as everyday coaches. They hold everything together, help keep us focused and moving forward, and allow us to lift others up by investing in their potential.

We are coaches in every aspect of our life, every single day, and we don't even realize it. We are always influencing and developing the people around us.

"Leadership encompasses coaching, teaching, mentoring, and motivating," explains Major General Uberti. "Everyday coaching involves creating an environment where everyone can reach or exceed their potential. This speaks to knowing when to let something go, and when to stop and revisit it. Some mistakes self-correct. Others don't. An effective everyday coach can create a 'teachable moment' and help their people recognize what's happening and how to fix it."

* * * * *

Everyday coaching strategies. Coaching is about far more than diagramming and executing plays or business plans. Together we're beginning a journey toward mastering aspects of influencing others that will help us become successful everyday coaches in every aspect of our lives. In the next sections we'll explore what everyday coaching looks like in our everyday lives, including:

- Strategic ways to speak to create desired effects

- Tactics in motivation and inspiration

- Behavior modeling

- Effective communication with intentional body language and eye contact

- Power of influence and responsible influence tactics

- Strengthen empathic neural pathways to better recognize causes and effects of your actions in others

- How to create winning environments

- Creating rapport and conversational style

- Introspection for proactive engagement

- Unique learning styles and teaching strategies

- Social learning theory

- Fixed vs. growth mindsets

After-Action Review

- Inspiration and motivation are closely intertwined, almost like a braided rope.

- Everyday coaching is influencing others to do something we want them to do because they want to do it.

- Inspiration and motivation separates the great teams from the good teams, and great everyday coaches from all the other coaches.

- If inspiration is establishing our compelling 'why,' then motivation is the day-to-day promotion of that initial inspiration. It's consistently taking the action needed to pursue our 'why.'

- When our 'should do' and 'want to do' become the same, our inspiration and motivation join forces.

- We are coaches in every aspect of our life, every single day, and we don't even realize it. We are always influencing and developing the people around us.

- Inspiration and motivation hold everything together, help keep us focused and moving forward, and allow us to lift others up.

PART 3
CONVEY

– Remembering and promoting our "why"

CHAPTER 20

"TRANSFORMATION IS EVERYONE'S JOB": THE STORY OF DR W. EDWARDS DEMING

Dr. W. Edwards Deming influenced American business more than almost any other individual, and yet today he's largely unknown to most people. Born in 1900, he inherited his lawyer father's penchant for learning and his pianist mother's love for music. His frugal upbringing influenced his belief in not wasting anything.

Deming attended the University of Wyoming, earning while he learned by working as a janitor and a soda jerk, among other jobs. In 1921 he earned his Bachelor's degree in electrical engineering. He taught engineering and studied mathematics at the University of Wyoming, and in 1922 taught physics at the Colorado School of Mines. In 1925, he received his Master's degree in mathematics and physics from the University of Wyoming. On the recommendation of a professor and mentor, Deming went to Yale on an instructorship to pursue his doctorate.

While studying at Yale, Deming spent two summers working on transmitters at Chicago's Western Electric Plant, where he witnessed the inhumane treatment of workers. While at Yale, he met Walter A. Shewhart of Bell Laboratories, who was applying statistics to manufacturing projects in a way that permitted workers to study and control variations. Deming would later adopt this as a fundamental principle of his life's work.

In 1928, Deming received his Ph.D. in mathematical physics from Yale. From 1927–1939, he worked for the USDA in Washington, DC, and also served as a statistical advisor for the U.S. Census Bureau. By 1935, Deming was responsible for courses in mathematics and statistics at the USDA graduate school. In 1940, he was asked to serve as an advisor for how the census was taken and results were sampled. This work had a major impact on the efficiency of the census process.

In 1942, Deming became involved with the U.S. war effort. He helped put together intensive eight-week courses to help train engineers, inspectors, and industrial people with or without math and statistical training and backgrounds. The courses began in 1943, and two years later had trained almost 2,000 people who carried that knowledge forward to influence others. This training strongly benefited the quality and volume of wartime production, with spectacular reductions in scrap and rework.

Dr. Deming became known for his "Deming Cycle": Plan (identify a problem) – Do (test potential solutions on a small scale) – Check (review the results) – Act (implement the best solution).

In 1946, Dr. Deming left the Census Bureau to go into private consulting practice. He became professor of statistics at New York University's Graduate School of Business Administration. He became "professor emeritus" at age 46.

In 1947, Dr. Deming was engaged by General MacArthur's Supreme Command of Allied Powers to advise on sampling techniques for a major census to be taken in Japan in 1951. The purpose of the census was to accurately assess war damage in order to develop a model for new housing.

In 1950, Dr. Deming was invited by the Union of Japanese Scientists and Engineers (JUSE) to teach application of statistics for quality improvement. Pre-Deming, the efforts were best described as "Aim Without Method." Dr.

Deming gave a series of a dozen lectures attended by Japan's top business leaders, government officials, professors, and students.

On 13 July 1950, Dr. Deming met with 21 of Japan's top business managers. This dinner meeting was a key turning point in revolutionizing Japanese industry. Deming told them if they followed his recommendations, they would capture markets the world over in five years, a stunning feat that actually began happening within four years.

Why did the leaders listen?

1. Their need to find a way to improve exports and bad image

2. Deming's connection with JUSE leaders

3. His respect shown to them at a time when their self-esteem was low

4. The interest he took in Japanese culture

In 1950, JUSE established the Deming Prize, awarded to people and companies for excellence in research, disseminations, and application of statistical quality control methods. The award recipient list reads like a Who's Who of Japanese companies: Toyota, Komatsu, Ricoh, Toshiba, Bridgestone, and Matsushita. (The equivalent U.S. prize, the Malcolm Baldrige National Quality Award, named for businessman and Secretary of Commerce Malcolm Baldrige Jr., wasn't established until 1987.)

In 1960, Dr. Deming was awarded the Second Order Medal of the Sacred Treasure, the highest award Japan can bestow on a foreigner, by the Emperor of Japan.

Twenty years later, on 24 June 1980, NBC aired a documentary entitled "If Japan Can, Why Can't We?" that did in the United States what the 13 July 1950 meeting did in Japan. Industry leaders sought out Dr. Deming's wisdom, and among many others, Deming's new approach to teamwork helped Ford Motor Company do a complete organizational turnaround.

At age 80, Dr. Deming began delivering what would become known as his famous four-day seminars around the world, and he continued that into his 90s. In 1987, President Ronald Reagan presented Dr. Deming with the National Medal of Technology. Dr. Deming died 20 December 1993, generously giving of himself and his wisdom up until the very end of his life.[26]

* * * * *

CHAPTER 21

WHAT DOES CONVEY MEAN?

We convey an object by carrying it to a place, and we convey messages or information by serving as a channel or a medium. We convey an idea or a process by making it known or understandable to others.

How does "convey" relate to everyday coaching? Convey is how we remember and promote our "why." Henry Ford's conveyor belt system revolutionized automobile production. Parts were created in mass quantities, then brought to work stations. Car chassis were transported by conveyor belts to various work stations within the production factory. This process reduced the amount of time workers spent retrieving parts from other places. The assembly line model decreased production time and increased profits. Ford pioneered the concept of "mechanize and customize" – basic car model bodies could be customized with components of the customer's choosing.

Conveyance becomes a matter of precedence: what needs to happen first? What can be completed at each station, and how long should it take? The first model, testing the conveyance method, takes the longest to produce. As the process of conveyance is studied, evaluated, and refined, production and quality accelerates. We learn what to focus on, and what type of variation from the standard is acceptable.

Dr. Deming developed the Deming Cycle, a proven approach to continual learning and improvement of a product, process, or service. It's useful to us as everyday coaches as we adjust our goals, change our methods, reformulate our theories, and broaden the whole cycle from a small experiment to a larger plan for implementation.[27]

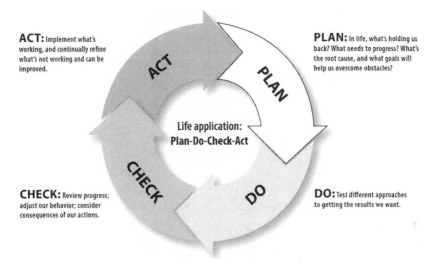

ACT: Implement what's working, and continually refine what's not working and can be improved.

PLAN: In life, what's holding us back? What needs to progress? What's the root cause, and what goals will help us overcome obstacles?

Life application:
Plan-Do-Check-Act

CHECK: Review progress; adjust our behavior; consider consequences of our actions.

DO: Test different approaches to getting the results we want.

Credit to W. Edwards Deming Cycle

As everyday coaches, we're not producing cars, robots, or identical products. But our product – our people – reflects how effectively we convey our "why." Every person is a unique individual with personality, talents, and tendencies. Recognizing the ways in which we most effectively remember and promote our "why" means focusing on what works, and what can be refined and improved. It means we aren't constantly using our time, effort, and energy starting over and searching out parts, or in the case of everyday coaching, searching out methods and approaches. We draw from a reliable resource of what's known and what works, and put that to work in our lives and the lives of our people.

Keys to Remembering Our "Why"

Pennsylvania's Levittown is an example of assembly-line logic applied to homebuilding. McDonald's restaurant is an example of assembly-line logic applied to food preparation and delivery. Hitsville U.S.A. is an example of assembly-line logic applied to music production. And The Everyday Coach is an example of assembly-line logic applied to coaching and mentoring. The Everyday Coach approach inspires us to recognize, apply, and practice the truth of everyday coaching in every aspect of our lives.

These are the keys to help us remember and promote our "why":

- fun

- knowledge

- message *(what* we communicate, not *how)*

- scars

- candor

- fitness

CHAPTER 22

KEY #1: FUN, AND WHY IT MATTERS

Dr. Deming opened his seminars by saying, "Why are we here? To learn and have fun!"

The Fun Factor. Early "sports," like unstructured playtime and pick-up games at the park or gym, are played for fun. Why do most kids drop out of team sports? And what's the main reason they continue to play? The answer is the same to both questions: "fun."

Physical literacy. Do you know that three out of four adults aged 30+ who play sports today also played sports as school-aged kids? Just *three percent* of adults who play sports now didn't play as kids.[28] Think about the value and lifelong benefit of "physical literacy" – learning and practicing basic movements like running, balancing, hopping, skipping, jumping, dodging, gliding, falling, lifting, swimming, kicking, throwing, and catching. These types of skills are best acquired by trying out a variety of sports rather than focusing exclusively on just one.[29]

CHAPTER 23

FUNDAMENTAL ELEMENTS OF FUN

Beyond inspiration and motivation, there are four fundamental elements we need to integrate into every game, practice, drill, activity, and decision we make as everyday coaches. They are: safety, energy, retention, and fun, also known as SERF. At first glance they seem specific to sports, but in reality, these elements permeate every aspect of our lives.

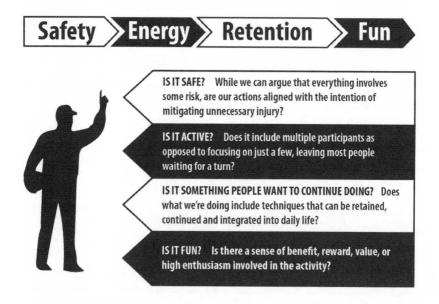

Safety > **Energy** > **Retention** > **Fun**

IS IT SAFE? While we can argue that everything involves some risk, are our actions aligned with the intention of mitigating unnecessary injury?

IS IT ACTIVE? Does it include multiple participants as opposed to focusing on just a few, leaving most people waiting for a turn?

IS IT SOMETHING PEOPLE WANT TO CONTINUE DOING? Does what we're doing include techniques that can be retained, continued and integrated into daily life?

IS IT FUN? Is there a sense of benefit, reward, value, or high enthusiasm involved in the activity?

How do we define fun? According to Dr. Amanda Visek, fun has four fundamental tenets: social, internal, external, and contextual. Dr. Visek's Youth Sports Ethos builds on those four tenets, and they are paramount for maximizing fun experiences.

1. Being a good sport (social)

2. Trying really hard (internal)

3. Positive coaching (external)

4. Practices and games (contextual)

These four tenets set the standard for fostering fun and provide 28 singular ideas that are directional beacons for promoting a culture of fun without sacrificing individual and team achievements.

Dr. Visek's Fun Integrational Theory, or FIT, captures 81 suggestions to improve the "fun" experience. FIT blueprints known as "fun maps" help us understand what's fun in youth sports and how best to foster fun experiences. They're organized into "fun factor" categories like games, team friendships, learning and improving, practice, trying hard, mental bonuses, being a good sport, team rituals, swag, game time support, and positive coaching. The "fun maps" illustrate how the fun factors are all inter-related, and which are considered of greater or lesser importance.

For more information: "The Fun Integration Theory: Towards Sustaining Child and Adolescent Sport Participation."

Fun Beyond The Field. Dr. Visek's fun-determinants aren't limited to athletics. The "fun factor" applies to activities like working together on a challenging project, playing a musical instrument or singing in a choir, and participating in virtual or real-life opportunities that involve learning, improving, rituals, trying hard, and positive coaching. We've seen videos of audiences captivated by people participating in a "flash mob" musical performance in unexpected settings. Are the participants and the observers having fun? One look at their delighted expressions tells us they are.

The distinction between "misses" and "failure." Fun allows us to distinguish between "misses" and "failure." In the 1995 movie *Mr. Holland's Opus*, Gertrude, a young music student, despairs of ever mastering the clarinet. Everyone in her family is good at something, and she feels the weight of their accomplishments and expectations hovering over her. Constantly comparing herself to them, she never quite measures up. "I just want to be good at something," she says wistfully. Her music teacher, Mr. Holland, asks her a simple question: "Is it fun?" He touches a needle to a record album, plays a piece of music for her, a few bars of the popular song "Louie Louie," and asks her why she likes it. Her answer: because it's fun. He asks Gertrude what she likes best about herself, and she self-consciously replies, "My hair. My father always says it reminds him of a sunset." Mr. Holland says, gently, "Play the sunset." And then, after pausing a single beat: "Close your eyes." And Gertrude closes her eyes and plays the feeling she has when her father comments on her beautiful red hair, halting at first, and then with growing confidence.

CHAPTER 24

ACCENTUATE THE POSITIVE (EMOTIONS)

While we have extensive research on the study of negative emotions, we know a little less about positive emotions. Researcher Dr. Barbara Frederickson offers a few reasons for this:

- They are less easily differentiated and harder to recall than negative emotions.

- Psychology studies problems, and positive emotions aren't usually associated with problems.

- Models of emotions are built on prototypes, and positive emotions do not exactly fit the model with a specific action tendency.

The Broaden and Build Theory

Enhanced health, survival, fulfillment

Building enduring personal resources (e.g., social support, resilience, skills and knowledge)

Novel thoughts, activities, relationships

BROADENING

Produces more experiences of positive emotions, creating an upward spiral

POSITIVE EMOTIONS

After Dr. Barbara Frederickson

Broaden and Build at Play. "Through play, kids build physical, intellectual and social abilities, as well as grounds for clear communication. Play also encourages exploration, which is the base for knowledge and personal growth."

Broaden and Build at Home. "Feeling contentment allows people to expand their world view and the view of themselves, which later leads to better social relations and skills. …[I]n close relationships, it promotes cycles where all of these can be experienced."

Broaden and Build at Work. "Creating a safe environment and company culture, encouraging employees to experiment without fear of repercussions for failure, and giving employees the opportunity to work on new and challenging projects, allows organizations to cultivate the positive emotion of 'interest.'"

Dr. Frederickson concludes, "Organizations that apply broaden-and-build findings to their management practices and culture are likely to find many positive impacts."[30]

Learning creates connections. We can use rational thought to down-regulate emotional centers. Practicing skills over time can lead us to a different approach. And once we learn something, we can't unlearn it. Our emotional connections, sometimes made subconsciously, influence our beliefs and our message to others.

Overcoming "I Can't!" When stress (in the classroom, at work, or at home) escalates, it's often because what we're doing seems irrelevant or too abstract. We despair of ever succeeding or mastering something, and often say, "I can't. I just can't do it!" However, if we can help make the essential connection between what we're doing and why it matters, that can help reduce stress and re-engage our people in the process.

Our goal as everyday coaches isn't to totally eliminate stress in the lives of our people. But offsetting stressful situations with things that are more positive can influence them toward success. Working really hard and following that with a brief break or respite like a three-minute vacation can generate the needed energy and focus to regroup and continue working really hard.

Remembering past successes motivates us to try harder to achieve more. If we are engaged in a challenge, whether on the field, at work, or at home, and know we have a meaningful part in figuring out a solution, and can even choose how we evaluate or report something, our motivation increases, our stress diminishes, and we learn to be more accepting of errors, motivated to try again, and less self-conscious about asking questions.[31]

CHAPTER 25

KEY #2: KNOWLEDGE

"Know yourself." Socrates' command is both deceptively simple and incredibly difficult. We can't effectively coach others unless we truly know, or commit to know, ourselves. As Cedric King says, "To be a great leader of people, you've got to be a great leader of YOU."

Much of what we know about ourselves is rooted in our feelings, intentions, and behaviors. What are our triggers? Why do we get aggravated by the things we do? How do we usually respond to stress? How do we handle criticism? What qualities in other people do we typically find annoying? What gets us excited? What do we consider a good use of our time? Our self-knowledge is easily influenced by fatigue, dehydration, and hunger. Ever heard someone described as "hangry"? How self-aware are they in that state?

In order to influence outcomes, we have to learn to accurately observe ourselves as well as our people. Coaching, in sports and in life, is emotional, and emotion is critical. As everyday coaches, we need to remember that our emotions, choices, and actions affect our people.

Know Your People. Think you know your people? Think again. Your players, other coaches, administration, parents, coworkers, colleagues, clients, casual interactions...how intimate is your understanding of what motivates them? What crushes them? As everyday coaches, it's vital that we have some level of knowledge of every single person in our coaching sphere.

"Know what you expect," says Jack Talley. "Don't bring the competition into the conversation. Talk about the desired action, not the undesired action." He encourages us to think about how we treat people and how we've been treated. Then, he suggests, think about where we want to be in a year. "You learn something from everyone," he points out. "How to act, and sometimes how not to act. You can choose your attitude, and choose your friends. People with good attitudes can lift you up, and people with bad attitudes bring you down. Choose to do the things you want other people to do."

Know Your Craft.

- **Be curious.** The practice of everyday coaching is exactly that. We are always learning. Be curious. Ask questions. Recognize while there is value in what we've learned, we don't have all the answers. There's always something new we can discover and implement: new techniques, skills, equipment, and approaches. The hallmark of maturity is a willingness both to listen and to learn. Get in the habit of asking, "What don't I know about this yet?" Don't just rest on what you do know. Relentlessly pursue what you don't know yet.

- **Be a student.** A little advice learned from a drama coach, according to entrepreneur and founding partner of Minute Man Restaurants & Matchbox Food Group (Washington, DC) Perry Jobe Smith: First, learn your lines. Then, focus on your connection with the other actors. In coaching, first learn your role. Then focus on your connection with your teammates and opponents.

- **Be an expert in your field.** While we're committed to continuing to learn and improve, we also want to become experts in our field.

In his book *Outliers*, bestselling author Malcolm Gladwell says to become an expert takes 10,000 hours (or approximately 10 years) of deliberate practice. What does that mean? Putting in the time alone isn't enough. Deliberate practice, according to programmer and author Kathy Sierra, is working on a skill that requires one to three practice sessions to master. If it takes longer than that, we're working on something too complex. Once we master this tiny behavior, we can move on to practicing the next small task that will take one to three sessions to master. Repeat this process for 10,000 hours. That is deliberate practice. And that is the path to expertise.[32]

- **Ritual and Routine.** Knowing ourselves, our people, and our craft can help us build into rituals and routines that help us and our people know what to expect in a situation.

  "Rituals ground us. They tell others we are someone they can work with," says Perry Jobe Smith. "Understand how to coach with intention. Get inside your players' heads and settle them through ritual. Repeating ritual behavior sets a common code and demonstrates expertise.

  "One coach's daughter decided to try out for her high school track team. She knew her preferred sport was the shot put. By showing the track coach her pre-throw rituals, she demonstrated that she knew the importance of setting herself up correctly."

Know Your Truth. A key component of self-knowledge is knowing our weaknesses and blind spots. Where do we need help? According to entrepreneur and former Notre Dame and University of North Carolina men's basketball head coach Matt Doherty, sometimes our biggest strength is also our biggest weakness.

We can enlist our brains as useful tools. The simple act of pausing and reflecting before reacting can increase our mindfulness and help us better regulate our emotions. We can also strengthen our ability to both accept and deliver criticism. Empathy is an essential skill, putting ourselves inside the other person's mind and heart when they're criticizing us and doing the same thing when it's necessary to correct them. Asking ourselves not just "how does this sound or feel?" but "How does this sound or feel...to them?"

CHAPTER 26

THE FOUR "KNOWS" OF EVERYDAY COACHING

Coach Doherty related four "knows" that are essential for anyone in a leadership position. They are relevant to us as everyday coaches as well.

Coach Matt Doherty's Four "Knows" of Leadership

The first "know" of leadership: **Know yourself**. What are your strengths and weaknesses? Where do you need help? Personality and skill assessments can be very helpful here, and surrounding ourselves with people who complement our strengths and weaknesses is essential. As an ENTJ, I was excited to learn I was elite – only 8% of the population has this makeup. Then I realized, no, that means 92% of the population doesn't think like me! It's good knowledge to have.

Know your team: your staff and your players. The same tools that help us know ourselves also help us figure out our people's personality strengths and weaknesses.

Know your industry: be an expert in your field. Continue to learn and improve and build on that knowledge at the same time you're asking your players to get better.

Know the truth. Most leaders don't mine for the truth. You're surrounded by people who are kissing your butt. They tell you what you want to hear, and talk about you behind your back. You're going to find out the truth sooner or later. Find it out sooner. Don't isolate yourself. What are the players thinking? What is the administration thinking? What is the word on the street? The truth is not a distraction. Know the truth. It's based on perspective (influenced by it).

Coach Doherty tells us to learn to expect bad news and manage it correctly.

Create a system where people will bring you the bad news. Reward and praise them for doing that. Create a culture of openness and trust. "We need to manage this. Any ideas on the best way to handle it?" Ask the most junior person their opinion first. They are the most closely related and recently connected to the team and understand better how the players feel.

Create a safe place for your people to come to you with their problems. When someone tries to disrespect or take advantage of you, choose to step back and respond intentionally.

CHAPTER 27

KEY #3: MESSAGE

Effective communication (our message) involves both input and output. Input is what we take in: what we hear, observe, and perceive about someone's intent. Output is what we put out: what we say, how we act, and what we project, both intentionally and unintentionally.

It doesn't matter what we say; what matters is what our people hear. Psychologist Carl Rogers said, "Man's ability to communicate is a result of his ability to listen effectively." We are one holistic sensory organism; at any given time, we are taking in the room, visual cues, the sound (pitch, decibel, tone, vocabulary). We listen, observe, and feel intent – what's happening behind and beyond the words.

In addition to the obvious output of the words we say, beyond our words, we are constantly feeling and projecting intent. We may say and intend one thing, but our subconscious body language changes what we're saying into something else entirely.

"Ever heard of a sycophant?" asks Coach Doherty.

> An insincere flatterer whose words and actions are self-serving? People don't want to jeopardize their position by giving their real opinion. If we surround ourselves with sycophants, we're breeding an environment of lies and people pleasing. Imagine the answers we get when we ask, "Why can't we win?"

A lot of CEOs are bullies. They aren't secure in who they are. They want to have all the answers. This generates an environment of power jockeying and backstabbing. It takes a lot to stand up to a leader like this in a meeting. Leaders need to be secure. A lot of leaders have gained their position by being insecure. It has driven them to the top.

We can intentionally own our conversational tendencies and our listening style. Do we speak calmly and thoughtfully, or hold our words until we erupt in an outburst of exasperation and anger? Do we listen carefully, or are we already forming our response as the other person is speaking?

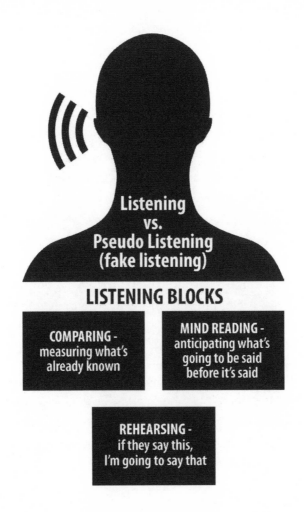

Listening
vs.
Pseudo Listening
(fake listening)

LISTENING BLOCKS

COMPARING -
measuring what's
already known

MIND READING -
anticipating what's
going to be said
before it's said

REHEARSING -
if they say this,
I'm going to say that

Forming our response in our minds while someone is speaking to us is a listening block called rehearsing. All of us do this, most often when we are being introduced to someone else for the first time. Have you ever been introduced to someone at a party, and immediately after shaking the person's hand, realize you have forgotten their name? If this happens to you often, do you shrug it off and say to yourself, "I'm just bad at remembering names?"

You are probably better than you think at remembering names. It's just that you were not listening to the person introduce themself. You were blocking their introduction by rehearsing your own. In your head, you were probably thinking about how your body language is portraying yourself, the tone of voice you were about to use, and the strength of your grip when you go in for the handshake. All of sudden you get the cue to deliver YOUR introduction. You stand tall, and with a kind yet firm grip, you shake hands while masterfully delivering a confident performance: "MY NAME IS [YOUR NAME HERE]. It is a pleasure to meet you."

You feel important, friendly, and happy to meet this new person. You think to yourself, "I bet this person and I could have a lot in common. What was their name again?" Then, for the rest of the evening you devise complex strategies to try and learn their name through clandestine conversation snooping. Imagine this: rather than rehearsal blocking, if you would have engaged by repeating their name back to them, you could have smoothly kickstarted a new friendship by giving them a genuine gift: your attention.

Other types of listening blocks

- Filtering – funneling everything through my own perspective and opinion; hearing what we want to hear or what we already know and believe

- Judging – close minded

- Dreaming – present in body, but mind is elsewhere

- Identifying – trying so hard to make a connection we miss the nuance of what's really being said; focusing on ourselves instead of the other person

- Advising – solving problems rather than hearing the whole story; fixing instead of fully listening. Coaches are already in the position of advisor, and sometimes we don't bother to hear completely

- Sparring – Verbalizing what may have been rehearsed mentally

- Being Right – determination to dominate the conversation

- Derailing – changing the entire direction of a conversation, intentionally or unintentionally

- Placating – saying what someone wants to hear in an effort to end or get out of the conversation; checking out so the other person will stop talking

What If I'm an Introvert? Not every leader is a gregarious, outgoing extrovert. The key in this situation is knowing where we have a deficit, whether that's knowledge, skill, or experience, and recognizing who has what we lack so we can enlist their help. Our goal isn't to change introverts into extroverts, but rather to provide tips on utilizing introverts' inner energy in an extroverted context for short periods. Some refer to this as being a 'situational extrovert.'

In the right setting, or with the right subject, and with the right goal, even an introverted person who's most comfortable outside the spotlight can shine for a defined period of time. The thing to remember? You're serving something greater than yourself. Jack Talley says, "What you're doing is bigger than a profession. It's life." Bill MacDonald agrees: "The better you are as a leader, the better all your people are going to be."

ENGAGEMENT
■ **Active Listening**
■ **Paraphrasing** – "So if I hear you correctly…" Summing something up in our own words to make sure the other person feels heard
■ **Clarifying** – "Is this what you're meaning?" Powerful antidote to daydreaming; restating what the other person said
■ **Provide feedback**
■ **Empathetic Listening** – Putting yourself in someone's shoes; wear their emotional vest – be where they are. Visualize being where your kids are. Coach to the inner 10 year old
■ **Listening with openness** – No filters, no judging, no blocks
■ **Listening with awareness** – Paying attention to the message context
■ **Fact check** – "Did you mean that…" Verify what's actually being said
■ **Meta-message assessment** – Listening with awareness to more than just words
■ **Beyond** – Body language, eye contact
■ **Commit to understand** – Not to agree or disagree; just try to understand what someone is telling us

Showing respect to others. "We show respect to others by allowing them to have a voice," says Coach Doherty.

> Listening is a talent. Listening indicates respect. It says, "He may not have liked my idea, but at last he gave me the chance to express it." When someone comes to us with a question, ask them what they would do. This imparts respect, input, and ownership. We have to be comfortable not having all the answers. Without input, morale suffers, fatigue sets in, and people leave.
>
> With practice we can separate our observant mind from our actual body. We can look at how our emotions are affecting us. And we can learn to regulate our emotions to make a better "R" – reaction.

Social learning theory tells us singular interactions affect everyone else around us. Points are made not only to the person we're talking to, but to everyone around us. Concentrate on creating a culture of openness and candor.

According to General Uberti, a good mantra to remember is, "I'm never the smartest person in the room." We need to be humble enough to recognize we don't know everything, and we can demonstrate a willingness to learn from everyone. As everyday coaches, we know it's not about the best player, it's about performing as the best team. How do you get groups of talented individuals to perform together? They can be great individually, but if they're not performing together, they won't achieve their collective goals.

> "We show respect to others by allowing them to have a voice." – Matt Doherty

—How do we accept and give criticism?

—How do we use candor appropriately without collapsing trust?

CHAPTER 28

KEY #4: COACHING SCARS

"When you're getting ready to perform at the highest level, before you perform in that stressful environment, you have to be comfortable in that environment," says Coach Williams. "You can't perform there if you haven't been put in those situations leading up to that. We are truly who we are under stress. We reveal our true selves. We all learn through the failures of people who don't handle stress well."

What is a Coaching Scar? How is it different from failure, which we discussed earlier? A scar is a wound that eventually heals, but leaves a permanent mark. According to Coach Doherty, coaching scars are moments in time we wish we had back so we could do something different. Every coach has coaching scars.

We could argue that becoming the head coach for University of North Carolina basketball is the pinnacle of coaching success. There may not be a more high profile coaching position in basketball, other than head coach of the Los Angeles Lakers. However, reaching the apex of personal or professional success does not exonerate us from scars we have left, nor does it mean we're incapable of leaving future scars.

Coach Doherty recalls the painful memory of one player who was referenced in a media article as a "role player."

The article was largely favorable, but the player referenced didn't like the article. We talked about the article before the game. During the game he may have made a mistake or taken a bad shot or something. It got heated in the time out, and I made reference to the conversation he and I had in the locker room.

As soon as the words came out of my mouth I knew I shouldn't be saying them. I'd broken a confidence and a trust. I could tell by his body language, the way his head went down, that I'd said something I shouldn't have. The next year was hard on him; he was the star player and we had a bad season. I don't think we ever connected again emotionally like we should have. He got into coaching, and I left for a couple of years and got back in. I'd see

Reaching the apex of success in our leadership career does not exonerate us from scars we have left or mean that we're incapable of leaving future scars.

him on the road and he'd avoid me. I'd go up to him and he'd hardly want to shake my hand. It was disappointing because you never want to have that relationship with a player. Later, I was in south Charlotte with my son, and he was there with his wife and baby. I approached him and said, "I wish I was a better coach for you at North Carolina." I extended the olive branch and apologized, but the scar still bothers me to this day.

What happened right before the coaching scar occurred during the time out? A frustrating sequence of plays. The "emotional lid" wasn't on tight. I reacted, and my "r" was bad.

We all make mistakes, especially as young coaches in high pressure situations. You hope as time goes on that things get better, that people start to understand decisions you made, kind of like having a conversation with your dad years later when you're grown. As our kids get older, they begin to understand the difficulty in the decisions we made. Growth helps. So does saying, "I'm sorry that happened."

Learning to manage our reactions. We have a moment in which we can recognize our triggers and realize we're becoming angry. It's a chance to use our brain as a tool and change the outcome of a situation. Preventing scars means preventing the wounds that cause them.

What things have the potential to really make us angry? When we recognize what those things are, and how we feel when they're present, we can step back and visualize a poor outcome to the situation, and a good outcome to the situation. Apathy and laziness in others is a trigger for me. I recognize it in others because I've experienced it personally. Ultimately, I don't want someone else to be apathetic and lazy. It's better for me to control my reaction, down-regulate my frustration, be empathetic and recognize that at times I, too, have been lazy and apathetic. How can I best react in a way that changes the outcome of this situation?

Improper reactions create wounds that will eventually heal as scars.

Improper reactions create wounds that will eventually heal as scars.

The importance of truth tellers. Coach Doherty says,

> We're in a circle. When we go outside the circle, scars are created. Truth tellers (trusted advisors) tell us where we need help and when we need to rein it in emotionally. Have a signal to tell your truth teller when to take over so you can step away and dial the rhetoric back. It helps you keep from crossing a line. That can be very difficult in the face of intensity, but it's based on trust. I had an assistant coach who knew when I grabbed the bridge of my nose in practice, I walked away and he took over.

"Learning about emotional intelligence makes us better coaches." – Matt Doherty

There's no formal training in leadership, and definitely not in coaching. Lawyers talk about legal practice, doctors talk about medical practice, and we should be talking about leadership practice. For example, aircraft manufacturing companies use simulators that allow them to test their products before they're sold to an airline, filled with passengers, and put into situations where lives depend on their safe performance. We need leadership simulators to help us learn to manage our responses and emotions in emotionally charged situations. This helps us learn emotional discipline and makes us more effective leaders. Learning about emotional intelligence makes us better coaches.

We can prevent future scars by recognizing our triggers, down-regulating our emotions, and pausing and reflecting to assess the context and the best course of action to achieve our intention. Still, sometimes our emotions take over, and we allow our reactions to escalate.

What do we do if we realize we may have created a scar? Being open to our mistakes, acknowledging them and trying to make amends is a marker of true coaching success. It's a long, long road.

Managing our own Reactions and Outcomes.

Knowing our triggers. We all experience both negative and positive triggers. Whether it's driving in heavy traffic or bad weather behind uncertain drivers, being peppered with constant questions and complaints, or watching someone continually give less than their best effort, it's essential that we're aware of what frustrates us personally and how our own reactions influence the entire situation. Knowing our triggers allows us to recognize and respond preemptively to situations that cause a bad response in us and in our people.

Expect events that set off our triggers. Anticipate how we'll recognize those situations and respond before we're in the situation. We can practice leadership by putting ourselves in situations that allow us to improve our responses.

We set the tone. As everyday coaches, we are much more responsible for our reactions and their outcomes. Everybody looks for a coach to throw down a headset in disgust at a blown call. Everybody watches an instructor whose student is challenging authority in the classroom or in the hallway. As coaches, even when a spontaneous outburst is imminent, we choose our reactions and the influence they generate. We aren't just victims of our own split-second reactions. We can learn to recognize triggers and manage our own reactions, and remember that we have a responsibility to respond thoughtfully and intentionally. This is something we can learn to do, not just an ability we either have or we don't. It takes practice every day in every situation.

As coaches, even when a spontaneous outburst is imminent, we choose our reactions and the influence they generate.

Every interaction is an opportunity. This is an opportunity to learn and grow. The best, most experienced coaches are able to effectively handle the most complex, stressful human situations. Instead of avoiding conflict and the potential to fail, we can learn to see this for what it is: an opportunity to get our misses up. Embrace the situation, do our best, and recognize that continually avoiding something is not going to get us where we need to be when it comes to dealing with stressful situations in our lives.

CHAPTER 29

KEY #5: CANDOR

Writer Peggy Noonan said, "Candor is a compliment; it implies equality. It's how true friends talk." As everyday coaches, when we speak with candor (compassionate honesty) we can set our people up to succeed. When the compassion is missing, we can set our people up to fail.

Candor promotes respect. How? By setting prior expectations, using compassionate honesty, and keeping our focus objective, quantifiable, and measurable (focusing on facts, not feelings), we demonstrate our respect for our people.

Candor isn't sugar-coating the truth, it's telling it exactly the way it is. It's respecting feelings, but not avoiding what needs to be said.

"Candor starts at home," says General Casey. "It's an investment in the confidence of our people. It's integral to our team to feel safe enough to talk about what we did wrong and what we can do better."

Bill MacDonald agrees: "You are responsible for others' success. Acknowledge and celebrate successes, no matter how big or small." One thing to remember: it's essential to not make ourselves indispensable, priceless, or irreplaceable. Otherwise we never get a chance to grow into another position. Instead, focus on grooming others to be and do better than we are.

General Colin Powell says, "As the old adage goes, it's more important to be respected than liked. Sometimes you'll have to make tough decisions that not everyone will like. Prepare yourself for these moments by thinking through why you made the decision. Realize that part of your job is to 'sell' your decision. That's part of diplomacy. However, in the end, if others don't agree, don't be afraid to hold your ground. Exceptional leaders possess passion and tenacity. Dig in and make sure that the best solution wins!"[33]

The Role of Candor. Two of character development coach and CEO of Black 4, LLC Adam Silva's favorite phrases:

1. "Tell the kind truth." (As heard from leadership consultant Brian Jones.) It's incumbent upon us as coaches to never dim the light of the spirit in our players. If you cross a line, apologize, and figure out how to fix it.

2. "The beauty is in the struggle." We can get so caught up in the results that we forget the importance of the process.

Our record doesn't necessarily reflect our effort. This doesn't mean we should strive for mediocrity. We can give our best effort, and the playing field still isn't level. But regardless of the outcome, if our emphasis is on process, we can still grow as people, individuals, and as a team, and growth in those areas is success, not failure.

Don't challenge someone's character. Get to know the people in your organization. Are their mistakes character-driven or circumstance-based?

Candor isn't brutal honesty. It's the kind truth. Compassionate honesty develops respect, and speaks to a person's high moral character. It builds and strengthens relationships by allowing us to focus on a cause greater than ourselves.

"We've heard the phrase 'devil's advocate,' and perhaps even used it ourselves," says Coach Silva. "It's often a preface for telling someone something they haven't considered or don't necessarily want to hear." The devil's advocate was once an official position within the Catholic Church, some-one appointed to question a candidate's saintliness prior to sainthood by suggesting natural explanations for miracles and human or even selfish motives for deeds described as virtues.[34]

> Don't be the devil's advocate. Instead, be a loyal adversary. Engage in productive conflict. Own our skills as coaches, and utilize our power correctly. We aren't here to win a championship. We're here to develop young lives. Winning a championship is a by-product of a well-coached team.
>
> Tom Landry once said that coaching at the NFL level is about making players do what they don't want to do so they have a chance to be what they want to become. Being a champion means being above average. And being your best is what it takes to be better than average. There's a difference between being THE best, and being YOUR best. Some of the greenest, most inexperienced players simply need to be challenged and empowered. We as coaches need to recognize those players can do more than they have opportunity to do, and give them a chance to do it. When we're influenced to do more than we ever imagined, we awaken to ourselves.

Look at where someone is performing. Where can they be better? What potential can they be working toward? THAT is a constructive conversation.

Coach Williams' players love him because he follows through with what he says he will do. He tells his players specifically what to expect if they don't live up to their potential. He uses colorful language to create a dramatic effect, and he knows who to put his arm around and love up afterward. He knows he has 22 year old millionaires who have tendencies to slack and be dispensable if they don't live up to their potential. During one of my first interactions with him, he destroyed me in the coaches' locker room. I began to smirk in the middle of his tirade, looking him in the eye, because it was over the top. It was an all-time great rant. I knew what he was doing, and Gregg knew I knew and was recognizing what was going on. I said "Yes sir," took the wisdom and applied it. The smirk wasn't disrespectful; it was more an appreciation of the fantastic outburst. Later Coach Williams called me into his office and noted that I was applying what I'd learned as a result of that experience. The respect between the two of us persists to this day.

In his best-selling book *Winning,* former head of General Electric Jack Welch said, "A remarkable absence of candor in the workplace represents one of the most significant obstacles to companies' success. In a bureaucracy, people are afraid to speak out. This type of environment slows you down, and it doesn't improve the workplace." Instead, Welch called for developing a corporate culture that encourages and rewards honest feedback. "You reinforce the behaviors that you reward," he explained. "If you reward candor, you'll get it."[35]

Candor: It's uncomfortable. Some people avoid it. Others sugarcoat it. But we can choose to talk about tough subjects with compassionate honesty, knowing it's a necessary component of effective everyday coaching. Candor is not brutal honesty. It's not a negative, sarcastic, put-down commentary. It keeps the conversational focus on things that are objective, quantifiable, and measurable.

Our leadership is reflected in how we treat others and how we conduct ourselves. As leaders, our job is to set expectations and hold people accountable. Don't just tell it. Show it. Live it. Don't be afraid of losing friends, and choose to tell the kind truth, always.

—How do you use candor effectively?

—How can candor help you be memorable?

CHAPTER 30

KEY #6: FITNESS

Maintaining healthy physical, emotional and spiritual fitness enables us to think clearly, make proactive decisions, and become catalysts for desirable action. Have everyday coaches been successful while neglecting one of these points of fitness? Yes. However, by focusing on them, can they become even better versions of themselves? Absolutely!

The Role of Fitness in Everyday Coaching. "For leaders to be successful, fitness is critical," says Bill MacDonald.

> Not just physical fitness; also mental and spiritual health. They go together; one can't be good and the other bad. If we don't feel good, it's hard to do good work and make good decisions. Likewise, if we're depressed or overworked, it affects our physical health. "Be a whole person" means that our physical, mental, and spiritual fitness all work together, influencing our ability to make clear decisions. We can't overestimate the importance of good physical health.
>
> Physical and mental health go together. Feeling good physically will benefit you mentally, and feeling good mentally will help you physically and help improve your performance. Our goal is a balanced life. Work is important, but family comes first. Sometimes you have to work in the red for a while, and other times you work less and relax more. Balance is essential, both mentally and physically. Otherwise you're going to burn out.
>
> **How do we do this?** Our organization has a policy of requiring and paying for annual physicals. That's a benefit of lower health insurance costs to the employee. We pay half the cost of fitness club memberships for our people.
>
> Every ten years, we require people to take six consecutive weeks off. No e-mail, no calls in or out, this is a sabbatical. Travel, sit home, do anything you want, just relax. Do it when you're younger, not when you're older and have fewer options. No job worries. It's not a replacement for normal vacation time.

The Totality of Your Person. We perceive the world through the totality of our person. Our thoughts actually change our brain. We secrete hormones and neurotransmitters which actually reshape our brain and change our body state. Consequently, our body state influences our mind, which affects our thoughts, which then influences our body and our ability to act.

The word "Satori" means "the feeling of epiphany, the 'aha' moment." It's a Japanese Buddhist term for awakening, comprehension, and understanding. It is derived from the Japanese verb *Satoru* which means "to know" or "understand."[36]

When we practice things over and over, there eventually comes an "aha!" moment when things click. It's awkward at first, the process of learning something new or learning to do something familiar in a different way. Trust the process. Trust our awareness of enlightenment. Once we know something, we can't unknow it. When it comes to Satori, everyone has their own moment of enlightenment. That enlightenment gives us control over a situation. It allows us to stop and think rather than just reacting in the moment. As everyday coaches, we can and should lay the groundwork for Satori moments with our people.

Physical Fitness and Mental Fitness. If we're in the best possible physical shape we can be in, regardless of the sport, we're going to win more often than not. This isn't just true in sports. Our physical fitness also affects our mental fitness. According to Dr. Sarah Gingell,

> Exercise directly affects the brain. Regular exercise increases the volume of certain brain regions, in part through better blood supply that improves neuronal health by improving the delivery of oxygen and nutrients; and also through an increase in neurotrophic factors and neurohormones that support neuron signaling, growth, and connections.
>
> Of critical importance for mental health is the hippocampus – an area of the brain involved in memory, emotion regulation, and learning. Studies in other animals show convincingly that exercise leads to the creation of new hippocampal neurons (neurogenesis), with preliminary evidence suggesting this is also true in humans.[37]

—*When you have good thoughts, how does your body physically change?*

—*How does physical activity affect your state of mind?*

The Significance of Self Talk. We may have a negative message that replays in our head every time we make a mistake. As a child we may have been told, "You'll never amount to anything," or "You can't do anything right." When we make a mistake—and we will because we all do—we can choose to overwrite that message with a positive one, such as "I choose to accept and grow from my mistake," or "As I learn from my mistakes, I am becoming a better person." Mistakes become opportunities to replace negative views of who we are with positive options for personal enhancement.

Positive self-talk is not self-deception. It is not mentally looking at circumstances with eyes that see only what we want to see. Rather, positive self-talk is about recognizing the truth in situations and in ourselves. One fundamental truth is that we will make mistakes. To expect perfection in ourselves or anyone else is unrealistic. To expect no difficulties in life, whether through our own actions or sheer circumstances, is also unrealistic. When negative events or mistakes happen, positive self-talk seeks to bring the positive out of the negative to help us do better, go further, or just keep moving forward. The practice of positive self-talk is often the process that allows us to discover the obscured optimism, hope, and joy in any given situation.[38]

> "Positive self-talk is about recognizing the truth in situations and in ourselves." – Dr. Gregory Jantz, psychologytoday.com

Do our Emotions Really Affect our Physical Health? Studies on longevity tell us that emotional factors are far more potent predictors of a long, healthy life than factors like diet and exercise. According to these studies, those who remain actively involved in life, possess a sense of hope and personal agency, and can deal with loss by creating meaning, instead of getting depressed and hopeless, lived longer, healthier lives than their pessimistic peers.

Our emotions are full of information and, when we have access to them, can create a kind of internal guidance system. Allowing ourselves to fully experience our emotions allows us to grow and change. Denying, avoiding, repressing, or simply acting on our feelings without taking time for reflection contributes to emotional and physical illness, as well as interpersonal conflict. Since the creation and maintenance of close and sustained relationships with others is one of the greatest boons to health, the healthy expression of emotions (which is the glue to all emotional connections) can make or break these vital ties. Studies tell us "emotional intelligence" – the ability to accurately identify and appropriately express our feelings as well as being attuned to those of others – is absolutely essential for maintaining healthy relationships. As such, emotional intelligence is a key factor in health, well-being and longevity.[39]

—How can I better shape my own mental self-talk?

—Am I allowing myself to fully experience and reflect on my emotions?

—How can I influence positive self talk in others?

CHAPTER 31

LIFELONG FITNESS IN ACTION

One of World War II's most celebrated heroes came from an unlikely beginning. Louis Zamperini was known for causing trouble in his younger years before turning his energy toward running. He quickly became one of Southern California's top athletes and qualified for the 1936 Olympics.

In 1941, Zamperini enlisted in the Army Air Corps, and served as a B-24 Liberator bombardier. In 1943, he spent 47 days lost at sea after his plane went down over the Pacific, drifting over 2000 miles in an inflatable raft. Captured by the Japanese near the Marshall Islands, Zamperini was held as a prisoner of war for more than two years and mercilessly tortured by his captors. Given up for dead by the United States, Zamperini was liberated at the war's end in 1945.

Battling alcoholism and PTSD, in 1949 Zamperini turned to a life of faith after reluctantly attending a service conducted by a young preacher, Billy Graham. Transformed by forgiveness, Zamperini began to speak about his conversion around the country and started a wilderness camp for troubled youths. In 1950, Zamperini returned to Japan for the first time since his release from captivity and addressed the Japanese war criminals being held in Tokyo. Imagine forgiving and embracing people who had tortured you for years.

In 1998, just before the winter Olympics, 81-year-old Zamperini was invited to carry the Olympic torch through Naoetsu, the Japanese town where he was held captive at the end of the war. Louis Zamperini died at age 97 in 2014.[40]

Zamperini's physical, mental, and spiritual fitness sustained him through the darkest times of his life. They made it possible for him to move beyond his years as a prisoner and offer genuine forgiveness to his captors. Fitness played a key role in allowing him to heal and to influence others for good throughout the rest of his life.

Self knowledge can be learned. We can choose to be *mindful,* observing our tendencies without acting on them. We can choose *responsibility,* owning our actions and reactions without blaming others. We can also own *how we choose to see things.* And we can choose *acceptance,* noticing and accepting what comes, instead of being distracted and procrastinating.[41]

After-Action Review

- Fun allows us to distinguish between 'misses' and 'failure.'

- Four 'knows' essential for anyone in a leadership position: know yourself, know your team, know your industry, and know your truth.

- We show respect to others by allowing them to have a voice.

- Coaching scars are moments when our actions have hurt someone enough that they will never be forgotten.

- Candor is sharing the kind truth.

- Compassionate honesty develops respect, and speaks to a person's high moral character.

- Maintaining our physical, emotional and spiritual fitness enables us to think clearly, make proactive decisions, and become catalysts for desirable action.

PART 4
CREATE

– Realizing our "why"

CHAPTER 32

THE MAGIC OF MOTOWN

He started out working as a shoeshine boy, then became a newspaper carrier. He tried boxing, then songwriting, and he kept getting knocked down. Nothing was working. Finally he decided to get a "real job." In Detroit in the early 1960s, that meant working on the Ford Motor Company assembly line. And it was while working there that he perfected his songwriting ability. Berry Gordy, the founding father of Hitsville U.S.A., cut his creative teeth witnessing car components traveling around the factory on belts and conveyors. He observed everyone doing their part to create vehicles that made Ford a household name on the lips of the driving public.

"I based my business on the assembly line model," says Gordy. He was raised in an entrepreneurial environment, and his resourceful parents instilled their children with a sense of self-sufficiency and an understanding of business. They operated Burberry Co-op, a savings and loan business within the family, to teach their children how money worked. An $800 loan from the family bank got Gordy started as a music producer.

"I was a producer, a songwriter, all these things…but really, I was a teacher. I had to find songwriters to teach," he says. And teach, he did. "Berry was like a coach with a great young talented team, and everybody was trying to play their best game," says actor Jamie Foxx. The songwriters were not trained musicians, by their own admission, but Berry could sense what needed to happen to make something pop.

People began coming from all over to visit Hitsville U.S.A., arriving with their talents and dreams and hoping to join the Motown family. Many started at the bottom, doing whatever was needed, whether it was playing tambourine or answering telephones. They got their confidence, began to make music together, trusted the process, and the hits began coming out of the unassuming former photography studio on Detroit's Grand Boulevard.

Lead singer Martha Reeves (of Martha and the Vandelas), who began her career with Motown answering telephones, recalls, "Detroit was a unique place with its migration of people coming from the South to find work. There was music in the churches, the clubs, and even on the street corners, but it took a place like Hitsville to bring people together to collaborate. Everybody worked in the same spirit, in one accord, making music."

Musician Stevie Wonder came to Hitsville at age 11, and was instantly recognized as a young genius. He described Hitsville as a "musical Disneyland – young people getting our feet wet – it was a one-time musical event. And Berry made us great."

"Being a teacher means finding ways to unlock people's true potential," Gordy says. He gave people what they needed most – freedom within boundaries. "I gave them direction, not only in music, but in life. Pushing people but not making them feel like they were being pushed. People were competitive, saying, 'Beat me – create a better record than I have.'"

Gordy nudged his people to sharpen their musical and personal tools to be the best possible version of themselves, according to Martha Reeves. Hitsville even had an "artist development" division, overseen by his sisters and run by etiquette instructor Maxine Powell, to help artists learn choreography and presence – how to walk, talk, and do things gracefully. She helped groom people to appear around the world, reminding them, "It's not where you came from, it's where you're going."

"It wasn't me – it was magic," says Gordy. "I was committed to bringing the best out of everyone. Motown reflected the world. We still need music that speaks to and expresses our hearts, and causes us to say, 'that's the way I feel!'" Singer-songwriter Smokey Robinson, who named his oldest son Berry in honor of his lifelong friend, agrees: "Success belongs to everybody. We were fiercely competitive, but we helped each other. We were the Motown family."[42]

* * * * *

CHAPTER 33

CULTURE

Inspiration and motivation are the cornerstones of culture. What is culture? It's the cumulative sum of everyone's habits and actions within the organization. Culture is a dynamic, changing practice created through repeatable experiences, and it can change in a heartbeat.

As everyday coaches, if we're only talking about culture, and not intentionally practicing it, we're not establishing it. Talk is cheap. "What the coach does to inspire and motivate forms the basis for the culture," says General Casey. "Culture becomes the sustaining 'glue' that holds the organization together."

Think about the Motown story. The culture fairly crackled in the air like sparks. The talent, the creative energy, the opportunity to take something new and run with it, the chance to "get your misses up" and improve while proving yourself – all the elements were in place. "I gave them [musicians and songwriters] direction not only in music, but in life," says Berry Gordy. "Pushing people, but not making them feel like they were being pushed." Berry Gordy embodied the essence of everyday coaching.

> "Culture becomes the sustaining 'glue' that holds the organization together." – General George Casey

CHAPTER 34

FOUR THINGS TO KNOW ABOUT CULTURE

1 – *Culture affects everyone's experience, every day.* Whether it's a sports team, a work setting, or home life, our culture is shaped by what we see, hear, and say every single day. Much more than the major events and milestones, it's our everyday experiences that influence and define our culture. Those experiences can be negative: that funky, unidentified, unremedied smell every time we enter a building or a room, or a supervisor who would rather hide and avoid people than interact with them. They can also be positive: the always-friendly barista at the coffee shop, or the quirky quote on the felt letterboard when we walk into someone's office. Nicknames, call signs, and customs become traditions and legends that all affect and define our culture.

In the 2000 movie *Remember the Titans*, the story of the 1971 Alexandria, Virginia, T. C. Williams High School football team, the Titans overcame mighty struggles with integration both on and off the field to eventually bond as a cohesive team. Before one late-season game, their unforgettable entrance into the stadium and onto the field, complete with throaty team-led lyrics and lumbering, earnest choreography, left spectators and opponents startled and confused. There was no arguing with the evidence that despite their differences, the team had learned to function as one cohesive unit, and their unity gave them a competitive advantage on and off the field.

2 – *Culture is only determined in retrospect.* Johns Hopkins University head football coach Jim Margraff once said, "A redwood tree takes 100 years to grow, and 15 minutes to cut down." Culture is the exact same way. It's slow to build and can be destroyed in an instant. Culture statements are valuable, but it's how we live up to them every day that truly determines our culture. When it comes to culture, while it's true that big things matter, everyday things matter even more.

3 – *One person, or one action, can change the entire culture.* Consider the legacy of Dr. Larry Nassar, former USA Gymnastics national team doctor and osteopathic physician at Michigan State University. He's also a convicted sex offender. One person repeating actions over time contributed to a culture of sexual abuse. Despite the fact that they were building a culture of good things and good performances, the actions of one person undid that legacy and permanently tainted the culture of the entire program.

> *When it comes to culture, while it's true that big things matter, everyday things matter even more.*

4 – *Culture is revealed by what we do when things don't go the way we expect them to go.* The HBO show *Hard Knocks* captures Coach Williams screaming and cussing with outrageous hyperbole. What we don't see is how, prior to ranting and raving, *he explains to the team that he is going to do this.* Coach Williams intentionally creates and allows stress in order to reveal people's tendencies and give them the opportunity to change and handle that stress in a more effective manner.

As everyday coaches, this knowledge is essential. We need to know not only what affects the people we're coaching when things don't go the way we want or expect them to, but also how it affects us.

"Everything I do is premeditated," asserts Coach Williams. "I don't do things without a lot of thought. I don't go off unexpectedly. What is my intention? Assertive communication.

To me, assertive communication involves five distinctives:

1. information (WHAT)
2. punctuality; a timeline for changing behavior (WHEN)
3. recruiting; change the way something is being done (ENGAGE)
4. empowerment; it becomes the other person's idea (BUY-IN)
5. demanding/shocking; only used if the first four haven't worked

If #5 doesn't work, it's time to move on. The person not engaging and buying in gets replaced so the job is accomplished.

A word of caution. We can communicate assertively without being abusive. As an employer, when #5 doesn't work, it's time to part ways. As an employee, if we're experiencing too much of #5, it's time to leave. As parents, too much of #5 requires taking a completely different approach. #5 isn't where we want to live in any relationship or culture. We can be demanding and shocking without being mean, disrespectful or contemptuous. That's the differentiating factor that contributes to an abusive culture, and it is to be avoided.

—*What do we personally need to pay attention to?*

—*What is the intention of my actions, and is this being clearly conveyed?*

—*How are my small, routine, everyday actions shaping the culture of my family, work, and team?*

CHAPTER 35

ONE MESSAGE, MANY VOICES

"Culture is a belief system of accountability," says Coach Williams. "It's setting a specific standard of excellence and holding each other to that standard. It's the same message being communicated in many voices. That makes buy-in easy. It also means you can't say things without meaning them.

"Communicating standards and doing things consistently builds a belief system that translates into confidence. Confidence translates into faster reactions, better instincts, and accurate anticipation. It keeps everyone on the same page. And culture beats strategy every time."

"Culture beats strategy every time."
– Gregg Williams

CHAPTER 36

CULTURE IS THE CUMULATIVE SUM OF EVERYONE'S ACTIONS AND BEHAVIORS

Culture, Gore Company style. Consider the culture at the Gore Company. What do they do? In their own words, they create solutions for challenging environments. Gore products are used in medical implants, fabric laminates, and cable, filtration, sealant, membrane, venting and fiber technologies for diverse industries.

What does any of that have to do with their culture? Gore's founder, former research chemist Bill Gore, determined not just to explore new markets for his products. He also focused on assembling and inspiring a team of creative collaborators.

Gore conceived of the company as a "lattice" connecting every individual in the organization to every other. In traditional organizations, it existed as an informal network of relationships underlying the formal hierarchy. At Gore, there would be no layers of management, information would flow freely in all directions, and personal communications would be the norm. And individuals and self-managed teams would go directly to anyone in the organization to get what they needed to be successful.[43]

Gore's philosophy is that individuals don't need close supervision; what they need is mentoring and support. Each new associate is assigned a sponsor to decode the jargon, demystify the lattice, and circulate him or her among several teams, helping find a good fit between the associate's skills and the needs of a particular team. A sponsor makes a personal commitment to an associate's development and success. As the organization has grown, teams of sponsors have begun to meet annually to take a broader look at the possibilities for the associates under their guidance. Associates are free to seek out a new sponsor if they wish.[44]

How has this non-traditional model of corporate culture worked? Gore is consistently cited as an example of a successful and innovative company by many business and management experts. It's a privately held company with $3 billion in annual revenue. For more than 20 years, it's been one of *Fortune* magazine's "Best Companies to Work For."[45]

Gore's description of a sponsor echoes our definition of an everyday coach. Mentoring, support, personal commitment to others' success, and guidance are all key components of everyday coaching.

That being said, the lattice environment isn't for everyone. There are drawbacks. A lattice culture can leave people wondering who has the ultimate authority and makes quick decisions almost impossible. At some point, a leader has to have the opportunity to accept responsibility. Without a defined hierarchy or structure, no one is ultimately responsible for anything.

Getting feedback as a new employee from someone with more seniority is invaluable. A lattice culture creates a blurred path to figure out the business process or culture. It can take a very long time to figure out "that's just the way we do it here." We can't tell if we're making progress or just moving around.

In the absence of clear feedback, the process of inspiration and motivation falls apart. It may not be a matter of good or bad; it's a matter of knowing what we're getting into. Gore has a defined, unique culture, and very high employee retention. It takes time to assimilate into a lattice culture, and not every culture is for everyone. Think about the visual of "cult-ure": If your culture is "cult-your," it speaks to 100% alignment.

CHAPTER 37

THE MESSAGE OF CULTURE AND EVERYDAY COACHING

How do we develop a better culture? How do we inspire our people to think differently? Nobody is more determined to do this successfully than Josh Grapski, owner of hospitality company La Vida. "Eating together creates an emotional bond," he points out.

> We know that the environment we create, intentionally or unintentionally, sets the stage for people's moods. We constantly ask ourselves "What vibes and emotions are we creating?" What is our goal for this experience? We know our environment, our products, and our service combine to create an emotional experience. It's not just the food, but the experience that promotes connection.

"I wanted to take what I saw working with sports teams and apply it to my business," says Grapski. "If people are our primary focus, how do we develop a better culture? How do we identify or label it and help everyone embrace it?" La Vida sees peoples' experience with their family of restaurants as not simply going out to eat, but getting away and connecting with friends and family and the surrounding environment. From the color palette to the furnishings, the material the tables are made of, the tableware used to serve the food, the style and brightness of the lighting, the hand-selected background music, the menu design, and even the way servers approach tables, every detail contributes to the overall culture, impression, and experience. That level of attention to detail speaks to intentionality and authenticity, and generates a positive impression of the brand's overall culture.

What about the employee experience? How does that contribute to culture? "How do we encourage team buy-in so our people are happier and more efficient?" Grapski asks. "At La Vida, we believe a clean, organized environment sets the tone for attitude and expectation of what we're going to deliver. Our back of house environments are clean, organized, and efficient, but we also want to make the front of house spaces as inviting as possible to encourage our people to want to spend their time there taking care of guests."

CHAPTER 38

HIGH HUMAN SKILLS

What are "high human" skills? In coaching, and in life, we often refer to "hard skills and "soft skills." Hard skills are objective and measurable. How far can we throw? How fast can we run? How much can we lift? How well do we comprehend what we read? We can attach a number or a standard to them and use them as a unit by which we measure someone's performance, strength, or maturity.

In this book, we refer to "soft skills" as "high human skills." High human skills are things like our ability to connect with others, our demonstration of empathy, and all the ways we open ourselves up to understand and be understood. For example, listening to others' ideas even when they're different. Asking great questions. Thinking about how someone makes us feel, or about how we make them feel. High human skills can be perceived as less important. In reality, they are in the greatest demand.

Using high human skills is the only way to do something that stands the test of time. High human skill development influences success. The great news is that as an everyday coach, you already have what it takes to develop and use these skills successfully.

"Go Fix That Base."

Brigadier General John Michel, U.S. Air Force (ret.) served as Commanding General, NATO Air Training Command-Afghanistan; NATO Training

Mission/Combined Security Transition Command-Afghanistan; and Commander, 438th Air Expeditionary Wing, Kabul, Afghanistan. He is currently a business leader, speaker, best-selling author, and organizational change expert. He says,

"High human" skills are critical to being a good coach. In 2008, I was asked to be Commander at Grand Forks Air Force Base. The base ranked dead last in the Air Force as the worst in terms of domestic abuse, etc. The base had a long history of mission and it was BRACed (Base Realignment Closure Commission). That left people shaken because they had no idea what the future would look like.

During what would become the shortest motivational speech I ever received, I was told by a four-star general: "John, go fix that base. Thanks for making the trip."

Upon my arrival, I began asking questions, observing, and engaging people where they were at. John Kinney and his PDP (Professional Dynametric Program) allowed us to engage people in terms of their strength, stress, and satisfaction. That allowed me to quantify how stressed the situation really was. It gave me the ability to measure satisfaction and see where people were mismatched.

Within three months, we launched the largest scale PDP exercise ever, involving more than 2000 people. We used the results to build a plan and marshal resources. We evaluated at wing level, assessing where people were being mismatched and where their stresses were burning unsustainable energy. Where was satisfaction sagging? We did similar assessments at group level and squadron level. This gave us an at-a-glance peek into the overall organization.

Also within three months, the four-star general flew back to the base to see how things were going. Instead of taking him on the usual base tour, we took him to the hospital to introduce him to everything that wasn't working. That tour showed him how broken the human spirit was. Employing the PDP gave me that knowledge.

The general then asked the only question I cared about: "What do you need from me?" I responded, "$250,000 to get started, and we'll follow up with you afterward." He reached over to his aide, took out a checkbook, and a process that should have taken months cut right to the chase. I used the tool of PDP to create quantitative and qualitative measures, and people could see I had a plan to start turning things around.

I started putting people in the right places and used tools to engage people where they were. We started envisioning bold futures. We put resources into programs about relationship building and dealing with stress. People could see I was serious about making things better for them. I quickly learned we couldn't dream big enough and we determined to do the right thing, but we needed some data to get it started. PDP was a very important tool to illuminate the state of affairs so I could use the information to engage people and do something about it, like go to decision makers with a plan. I have never run into a decision maker that didn't act on a plan backed up by data.

"Tools used wisely unlock new possibilities." – Brigadier General John Michel

I was hated by a lot of folks because I didn't follow the rules, but you know how empowering it was when I went back to people with a plan for what was possible? Tools used wisely unlock new possibilities.

CHAPTER 39

TOOLS FOR TRANSFORMATION

There is tremendous strategy in using high human skills to change environment and culture. It's a powerful tool used to elicit the best from people. One of my favorite examples of this is Brigadier General Michel's Gratitude Café in Afghanistan.

[At the time I was there] Afghanistan was a very disempowered culture. When they saw we were serious about engaging, they were hungry for it. But how do you take fourteen different nations, with various language and cultural barriers, and a finite amount of time, to accomplish a mission?

I did two things. The first one we called a blog or a Sunday soundbyte. Every week, I released a 600–800 word blog about the type of high human skills required to be a good leader. How do you use your influence well? A book came out of that, a soft skill handbook, *The Art of Positive Leadership*. Something people could read wherever they were to understand how to be a good human. Wield your influence well, because you are an advisor to these Afghans and to each other.

Second, I knew people are social creatures. If we could get the social aspect right amongst ourselves, it would make us more effective engaging with our Afghan partners.

For months I'd been walking past a dilapidated trailer on the side of the road within our compound. I wondered, what is something that crosses all cultures and is universally accepted? Obviously, coffee. What if we leveraged coffee as a way or in a space where people can start their day over a shared cup of coffee in an informal way, all ranks, all cultures, just talking over coffee?

We did a self-help project renovating the trailer and we called it Gratitude Café. I established a series of rules on how it was going to work. No longer would I be involved in meetings before 8:30 a.m. Every day, 5 days a week, from 7:30 to 8:30 a.m. was coffee time in the middle of the compound at the Gratitude Café.

The only people allowed to make the coffee and serve others were the highest ranking officers on the compound. That was myself, colonels, and the chief master sergeant. We inverted the pyramid. It would have been easier to have a structure in which airmen made and served the coffee. The message we sent said that we were happy with power inverted because we're here to engage with you and we're going to do it by serving you. It quickly became cultish. We got more work done and had more real meaningful conversation and team building in that hour over coffee than in most of our other meetings throughout the day.

The second thing that happened was that different cultures wanted to volunteer because they had specialty drinks in their own culture they wanted to make and share with the whole compound. Guys from Greece said, "We want to make coffee on this Tuesday, because we have a special coffee we want to make for all of you." They felt they could make a contribution. Consciously and emotionally, we sent the message throughout the compound that we wanted to focus on human relationships first. If we could be good stewards of human relationships among ourselves, we could set a better example among our Afghan partners.

Gratitude Café was also used to tell a bigger story. Because we kept receiving supplies and things from the States, people opened up to the idea and began using social media to celebrate who was supporting Gratitude Café. People around the world wanted to be part of something bigger than themselves. They wanted to go "high human." Gratitude Café ultimately became a place where Afghans began to meet. They loved having access to their coalition partners and even began cleaning us out, taking snacks home to their families. We infiltrated the Afghan family unit, connecting at a much deeper level than we would have otherwise. The results were astounding.

Not once was there a mandate. The only mandate was that highest ranking officials would serve everyone else. We created an environment and construct of influence and let it take on a life of its own. People self-organized to carry the idea to its highest possible state.

"Greatness occurs when people believe their coach or leader has their best interests at heart. The measure of a real leader is what kind of environment they create or allow." – Brigadier General John Michel

How do I view leadership? The only role of a leader is to create conditions. We are responsible for creating an environment where people feel safe enough to show up and be their authentic selves and give their best. It means being open to ideas. Setting aside my agenda. Listening to what they have to say and how to include them. Having courage to do hard things. Bringing in tools or teaching emotional intelligence in a war zone in Afghanistan. My only job as a leader is to create the conditions to elicit the best in human conditions. Always look out for and realize the value of others.

I had the privilege of leading a team of people passionate about what they were doing. They needed to know that I had their best interests at heart - that is the desired response to leadership. The best leaders elicit this response. Greatness occurs when people believe their coach or leader has their best interests at heart. The measure of a real leader is what kind of environment they create or allow.

Changing the environment can change the culture from dysfunctional to stellar. Instead of engaging with warfare, we were there to help develop skills in our native counterparts. Some missions are transactional. Some are transformational, influencing generations.

All of life is high human work. The only thing that truly matters is the influence and impact we have on others. It's our choice to do it well or do it poorly.

People want to be part of something meaningful. They want to know they matter. When you focus on the high human element in every aspect of your life, every other aspect falls into place. This is how you influence and change society. In the process of growing other people, you're growing yourself.

"The terms 'leader' and 'coach' are synonymous," says Brigadier General Michel. "They choose to wield their influence wisely, with intentionality, for the purpose of eliciting the best in other people."

Mastering high human skills helps us become better versions of ourselves. Many of you who are military service veterans have already communicated your willingness to be other-centered. You've proved that you're willing to fight for and die for a cause greater than yourself. Everyday coaching is all about helping others meet their potential. It values the things you accepted as normal in your military life. It puts you in an environment you already know.

—*Are there people in your life who have helped you develop "high human" skills?*

—*What techniques can you employ to develop "high human" skills in other people?*

CHAPTER 40

THE SCARF MODEL

Neuroscience of leadership and executive coaching expert Dr. David Rock has developed a brain-based model called SCARF (an acronym for Status, Consistency, Autonomy, Relatedness, and Fairness). These words represent five key domains or triggers that influence our behavior in social situations. They activate the same threat and reward responses in our brains that we rely on for physical survival.

The SCARF model is most effective when we understand the people around us. What do others see as a threat? What reward do they most desire? Remembering that our brains are wired to seek pleasure and avoid pain, the SCARF model is particularly useful when we need to collaborate with, influence, or coach others, or when we need to provide training and feedback.[46]

Status. This refers to our relative importance to others. For example, when we're left out of an activity, we might perceive it as a threat to our status and relatedness. Research has shown that this response can stimulate the same region of our brain as physical pain. In other words, our brain is sending out the signal that our status is in danger. On the flip side, when we feel rewarded (for instance, when we are praised for our work), our brains release dopamine – the "happy hormone." We want more of that, so we seek out ways to be rewarded again.[47]

Consistency. The best NFL teams and college sports teams have figured out that consistency in schedule is paramount in building confidence within the players, the staff, and the team as a whole. This allows players and staff to know what to expect on any given day. Any needed changes are clearly stated well in advance. Perturbations in daily routine create uncertainty in everyone's mind.

Autonomy. Our sense of control over events; as Perry Jobe Smith says, the freedom to speak freely.

Relatedness. How safe we feel with others. Kathy Ciric, freelance television producer, says, "Create whatever you want to create, but connect with your people." Kathy is the epitome of great coaching. Memorable, inspiring and effective, she is a "high observer" who makes sense of how actors need to interact on stage. She is also adept at adapting, seeming to intuitively sense how best to handle individual situations with people. "You don't have very many lines," she told one actor, "but you have a very important role in this play." Actors need to listen, be engaged, and stay connected in the moment. "Effective coaches ensure their people understand they have a voice," says Smith.

Fairness. How we perceive fairness in the exchanges between people. "Morale will always stay high as long as everyone believes they're being treated fairly," says Coach Williams. "When someone perceives others are being treated better or worse than they are, you have to excise that. It's essential to keep everyone on the same page. It takes constant reevaluation to make sure everyone perceives they're being treated fairly, and constant reevaluation that the message is consistent, day to day and week to week. It can slip away if we're not tuned into it."

As a football coach, there are certain repercussions that will vary between players. For instance, being late to practice. If you have never been late to practice, you're a captain of the football team, you're a three-time All American, you score all of our points, and you've led this team, and you are unexpectedly late to practice, that repercussion will be different than if you're a freshman, you've been here two weeks, and you're trying to figure out where to go. As a freshman, your repercussion will be a little stronger to send you a clear message and help you figure things out. You have no demonstrated body of work to show your record, and therefore, the repercussions for being late will be fair, but not equal.

SCARF in Action. Gratitude Café is an outstanding social model of Dr. David Rock's SCARF model. When we catalogue things people are wired to want, things that resonate in positive ways, we are better equipped to assess and create a physical and emotional environment. Consider Gratitude Café within the structure of the SCARF model:

> **Status** - top side down, leaders are serving others.
> **Consistency** - five days a week, everyone's having coffee between 7:30 and 8:30 a.m.

Autonomy - Coffee and tea are the great equalizer; everyone can help create and control the menu offerings.

Relativeness - Everyone gets to relate to everyone else; equal access, opportunities exist here that don't exist anywhere else.

Fairness - Everybody knows where they stand and everyone has a voice. Everyone gets to speak their own truth.

CHAPTER 41

GROWTH MINDSETS AND FIXED MINDSETS

Growth Mindsets and Fixed Mindsets

Psychologist Carol Dweck is known around the world for her work on the psychological trait of mindset. She researches and describes two different types of mindsets, growth and fixed.

Growth Mindsets and Fixed Mindsets

GROWTH MINDSET

- Takes on challenges
- Unafraid to fail
- Trusts and enjoys the process; less concerned with outcome

Adapted from *Mindset: The New Psychology of Success,* Carol Dweck

FIXED MINDSET

- Believes traits like intelligence, talents, and abilities are set in stone - fixed, stationary, unchanging
- Documentation is more important than development
- Focused on the outcome or results, not the journey

Growth Mindset. "In a growth mindset, people believe that their most basic abilities can be developed through dedication and hard work

– brains and talent are just the starting point. This view creates a love of learning and a resilience that is essential for great accomplishment.[48]

Fixed Mindset. In a fixed mindset, people believe their basic qualities, like their intelligence or talent, are simply fixed traits. They spend their time documenting their intelligence or talent instead of developing them. They also believe that talent alone creates success – without effort.[49]

When you enter a mindset, you enter a new world. In one world – the world of fixed traits – success is about proving you're smart or talented. Validating yourself. In the other – the world of changing qualities – it's about stretching yourself to learn something new. Developing yourself.

In one world, failure is about having a setback. Getting a bad grade. Losing a tournament. Getting fired. Getting rejected. It means you're not smart or talented. In the other world, failure is about not growing. Not reaching for the things you value. It means you're not fulfilling your potential.

In one world, effort is a bad thing. It, like failure, means you're not smart or talented. If you were, you wouldn't need effort. In the other world, effort is what *makes* you smart or talented.[50]

Someone with a fixed mindset usually gives up when they can't solve a problem or achieve a goal. We hear words like "I can't" or "I never" or "It's too hard." Alternatively, someone with a growth mindset continually works to improve their skills, performance, and results, They know how things are right now isn't the way things will always have to be. The phrase 'not yet' is a fulcrum on which their future performance rests.

"If you want to get stronger, you've got to get your misses up." Remember Bill Starr's words? When you miss trying to reach a greater goal, the intermediate goal, which was once unobtainable, can become reachable.

CHAPTER 42

AWARENESS OF OURSELVES AND OUR PEOPLE

Most people want to have a positive impact, but they are out of alignment because they lack self-awareness. So many people walk through life completely unaware of the way they're affecting other people. We need to remember to own the responsibility for the power we all have to influence others. True servant-leaders recognize they are stewards of power and cultivate skills to wield that power wisely. Especially in sports, young athletes hang on every word we communicate.

Self-Awareness and Audience Awareness. It's important that we have self-awareness as well as awareness of the listener. With practice, we can learn to quickly assess our own mood, thoughts, needs, and reasoning behind what we're communicating to others. It only takes a few seconds to think about what we're really trying to communicate, and why, and how important our message is. Sometimes we might find our message has less to do with our audience and more to do with ourselves.

How Aware Are We? These questions are a way to evaluate what we're going to say before we put out something we have to own. As we become more aware, it does become more intuitive. We learn to read context and body language and better know what to say, to whom, and when.

How Aware Are We?

Self Awareness

These are questions to ask yourself:

- What is my current mood?
- What am I thinking?
- What am I seeing?
- What am I REALLY trying to communicate?
- Why am I communicating this?
- What are my needs?
- How important is this communication?

Audience Awareness

These are questions to ask yourself:

- What is their current mood?
- What is their body language telling me?
- What is the context of the communication?
- Are there extenuating circumstances that you know?

CHAPTER 43

COMMUNICATION AND EMOTION

Facial Expressions. There are eight universal emotions:

- joy and sadness

- acceptance and disgust

- fear and anger

- surprise and anticipation

Just eight. Four sets of opposites. They can be combined with each other and with levels of intensity to create an almost infinite number of emotion combinations. For instance:

- trust goes from acceptance to admiration

- fear goes from timidity to terror

- surprise goes from uncertainty to amazement

- sadness goes from gloominess to grief

- disgust goes from dislike to loathing

- anger goes from annoyance to fury

- anticipation goes from interest to vigilance

- joy goes from serenity to ecstasy

The Dalai Lama commissioned a book called the *Atlas of Emotions* to help us become more aware of our emotions and how we convey them.[51] It catalogues 10,000 different facial expressions and what they represent. Talk about nuance! It refers to a Facial Action Coding System, or FACS.

Wheel of Emotions

Emotions influence our health, performance, well-being, motivation, sense of fulfillment, and decision-making skills. It's important to understand and manage them.[52]

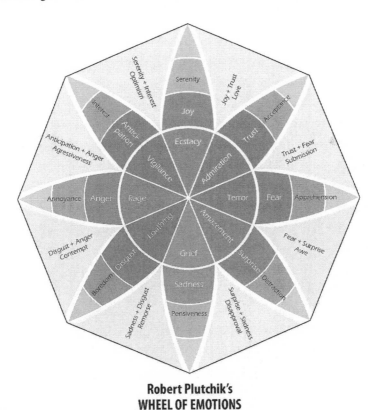

Robert Plutchik's
WHEEL OF EMOTIONS

While it's true that there are more negative emotions (shame, fear, sadness, anger, disgust) than positive ones (happiness, surprise/interest), both kinds are vital for our survival.

That's because our real emotions help us get what we really want. And by listening to the emotions we've been carrying around, but have been ignoring, we can release the stagnant ones and make room for new ones.[53]

Capturing and defining feelings. *The Dictionary of Obscure Sorrows*[54] is a digital compendium of invented words written by John Koenig. It's also accessible on YouTube. Some of the terms and definitions:

> **Agnosthesia**: *n.* the state of not knowing how you really feel about something, which forces you to sift through clues hidden in your behavior, as if you were some other person – noticing a twist of acid in your voice, an obscene amount of effort put into something trifling, or an inexplicable weight on your shoulders that makes it difficult to get out of bed.

> **Middling**: *v. intr.* feeling the tranquil pleasure of being near a gathering but not quite in it – hovering on the perimeter of a campfire, chatting outside a party while others dance inside, resting your head in the backseat of a car listening to your friends chatting up front – feeling blissfully invisible yet still fully included, safe in the knowledge that everyone is together and everyone is okay, with all the thrill of being there without the burden of having to be.

> **Scabulous**: *adj.* proud of a scar on your body, which is an autograph signed to you by a world grateful for your continued willingness to play with her, even when you don't feel like it.

The Role of Memory and Emotion. We all have two main memory systems, implicit and explicit. Our implicit memory houses unconscious processes like emotional and skeletal responses, learning skills and habits, and reflex actions. Our explicit memory stores facts, events, and things that require conscious awareness to recall.

We can have implicit fears without recalling the explicit experiences that caused them, like fear of clowns, fear of animals, and fear of heights. We may not explicitly remember the instance that caused us to fear something, but the physical and/or emotional reaction remains strong. One of my personal favorites: "I had a bad experience with sweet potatoes as a child," resulting in a lifetime grudge against an innocent and beneficial vegetable.

Pixar's 2015 animated movie *Inside Out* featured five prominent emotions: joy, fear, sadness, disgust, and anger. Told through the eyes of the five emotions and the life of an 11 year old girl, the movie's takeaway reminded us that emotions, even ones we perceive as negative, like sadness, are necessary for effectively dealing with life's ups and downs.[55]

CHAPTER 44

BODY LANGUAGE

There are no right and wrong answers when it comes to body language. Our bodies simply speak their truth. Regardless of our words, tone, or intentions, our body language is a true tell of our actions and reactions. With practice, we can learn to interpret and regulate the clues, both our own and those of people around us.

How we say: Body Language. "I can't hear your words because your actions are so loud." Have you ever observed someone in conversation from a distance great enough that you can't hear what's actually being said? What can you discern about what someone is really saying with their demeanor?

Think about Coach Herb Brooks talking to the U.S. Olympic hockey team in the story related previously. Walking slowly, speaking slowly, standing tall, head up, making steady eye contact. He was confident, in control, not anxious, nervous, or stressed. The room was tense, and he used the intensity to his advantage because he knew what was at stake. His face reflected intensity, but not anxiety. He used his voice tone and pauses for dramatic effect. Walking around, he addressed everyone. His body language mirrored his words.

CHAPTER 45

COMMUNICATION AND COMPARISON

Social Comparison. We live in a social construct of perspectives and opinions from different backgrounds that all have to coexist together. When we go to the supermarket, we're navigating a social chess game with unwritten rules about whose turn it is to go where, who's lingering too long or taking up too much space around themselves, who leads the way and who follows. Try cutting in line ahead of someone at the deli, pharmacy, or checkout and see how quickly the unwritten rules are enforced. And try letting someone go ahead of you, or even paying a few dollars toward their bill, and see what happens then. And that's just inside the store. Think about the "rules of the road," and the "rules of the parking lot."

We're learning and following social rules and coaching others every single day in every aspect of our lives. When our intent is to understand each other and come together, every relationship can improve. That intent can and should include a willingness to respectfully disagree while working toward common goals.

"Ego (concept of self) mixed with social media causes us to compare ourselves to others," says U.S. Army (ret.) Major General Tony Cucolo, who served as the Army's Chief of Public Affairs, Commander of the 3rd Infantry Division and Fort Stewart/Hunter Army Airfield (GA), and Commandant of the Army War College.

That's a big mistake, that is, to ask yourself, "What do others have that I don't?" Think about it: you are judging yourself against your mere perception of another person – based on what is probably an inaccurate snapshot – of that person in a certain place and a certain time. Really now…will you allow that to become your personal goal?

Comparing yourself to others is a natural human trait, but leaders need to know such individual practice can distract from desired organizational performance. Individuals and leaders must get control of it and keep it in perspective and in context. As everyday coaches, we do not compare our people to one another. One of the worst things a leader can say is, "Why can't you be more like…?"

If we start to lead and manage this way, based on comparison, it ends badly. I'd rather coach, teach, and mentor to a set of traits, skills and abilities the outfit needs – let us compare ourselves to a standard, not another human.

Often, we tend to drop the standard and say, "That is good enough," trying to get easy wins. We accept "okay." "We lower standards because we are scared to let people fail, or we worry how they will handle failure," General Cucolo says. Instead of lowering the standard for those reasons, we should say, "You fell short on this one; you didn't make it. This doesn't mean you are a failure; you just didn't meet the standard – let's work towards that. With more effort and practice, you will do it!"

Comparison and success. "Misplaced ambition and comparison to others can cloud and inhibit selfless service," says General Cucolo.

I would require officers for whom I wrote evaluation reports to turn in a simple, one-paragraph "definition of personal success" when they turned in their sheet of annual accomplishments. My only requirement was that whatever they wrote could not be connected to rank or a position. I coached them to see success as things such as, "to make a contribution in…" or "to have an impact with…" My thinking here is if your definition of success is connected to a specific rank or position, you disadvantage yourself. If success to you is billionaire, U.S. senator, and Nobel Laureate…what if you don't achieve any of those? Are you a failure? No! So, do not tie your definition of success to something like that…look, I told them, you might not be a senior commander or a General Officer, but the Army needs you and all your talents and skills and what you bring to the organization. It is always a good time to reevaluate why you serve or why you are doing what you are doing. This practice can be re-energizing, particularly for mid-career leaders. At some points of a professional life, old motivations have passed and have no place; regenerate new and relevant ones. What is your new motivation to continue?

Investing our best effort in the lives of others. Some of the world's greatest coaches are people we've never heard of. Some people reach the pinnacle of the coaching world, then intentionally step into a role others might perceive as "less than" – coaching middle and high school sports, for instance – because of the opportunity it offers.

"Coaching middle and high school track caused me to reinvent the way I view coaching," says Martin Rooney.

> Whatever you do that you find yourself escaping to, that you love so much you'd do it for no money, that should be the thing you're doing. Never be afraid to invest in yourself. Pay your dues.
>
> What makes the ultimate coach? Does what I do, teach, and train carry forward when people are coached by other people? That's the difference between saying, "I want to be the best coach ever," and "I want to invest my best effort in the lives of other coaches."

CHAPTER 46

COMMUNICATION AND CREDIBILITY

When we're communicating, there are four types of expression to remember:

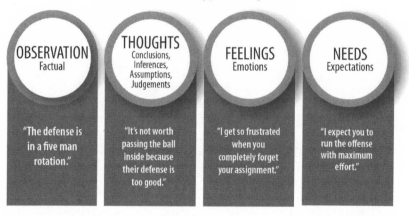

CREDIBILITY - Four Types of Expression

OBSERVATION Factual	THOUGHTS Conclusions, Inferences, Assumptions, Judgements	FEELINGS Emotions	NEEDS Expectations
"The defense is in a five man rotation."	"It's not worth passing the ball inside because their defense is too good."	"I get so frustrated when you completely forget your assignment."	"I expect you to run the offense with maximum effort."

As listeners, we constantly ask ourselves, "Why should I listen to this person?" People listening to us are asking themselves the same question. When we're communicating, whether we're speaking or listening, we can benefit from our awareness of the four types of expression:

Observations: (Factual)

- Be consistent, and explain contradictions. The world is complex and dynamic, full of contradictions and hypocrisy. "I observe this to be true; sometimes it's not."

- Admit when you are wrong or don't know something.

- Cite your sources of facts and observations. Where did you get the information you're sharing? Proper credit adds credibility.

Thoughts: (Conclusions, inferences, assumptions, judgments)

- Clearly articulate inferences, judgments, assumptions, theories, and beliefs.

- Explain your rationale.

Feelings: (Emotions)

- Eliminate blame and identification – never say someone is lazy; instead refer to behavior (gives a time frame).

- Say "I feel" vs. "You make me feel" – own your feelings; "I feel frustrated when this happens." As leaders, when we teach by modeling, we can say "I feel so angry when I watch you start to do these things. I don't want to be angry. Why are you doing this?" Other people won't change their behavior just so you can feel better. Remember how much power you're giving someone else when you allow them to be responsible for how you feel.

Needs:

- Eliminate blame and identification.

- Don't demand what you can't enforce – communicate expectations. No ultimatums. Ordering 200 grueling athletic drills known as "suicides" is neither realistic nor safe. Neither is setting unreasonable expectations that can't be accomplished or enforced.

- "My way or the highway" will leave you alone on the highway. You might get compliance, but without heart.

CHAPTER 47

COMMUNICATION AND OUTPUT

The "why" of our communication output is to project intent and establish credibility. But when communicating with others, there's another "why" to remember: the "why" of our listener. Our listeners are always asking themselves, "Why should I listen to this person?" Even more than our pedigree or our accomplishments, they care if we are communicating clearly and honestly with them.

Deliver the entire message clearly always. If we don't, we run the risk of people putting up communication blocks. Ask, "Who doesn't understand? I'm not trying to call you out. I'm trying to make sure everybody is 100% clear." This is essential to establishing and maintaining credibility.

Truth Mining. Who are we really? Ask questions, don't just give answers. Pull, don't push. Build confidence by remembering and highlighting past successes. Mine for the truth. The truth may be a lack of self-confidence. We can give our team confidence. Confidence is a fragile thing. Confidence building is a skill that can be developed. It's part of the art of coaching, and we can learn to refine our art by cultivating and developing it.

The number one impediment to effective organizations is poor communication. Words are drugs. When we say words, it literally causes a physical change in our bodies. Tone and word selection is critical (how language is given and received).

The Importance of Focus. "Are there things you'll do intentionally to create specific effects?" asks Coach Williams.

> When soldiers are standing at attention, they're creating the best picture of intense focus and everyone being on the same page possible. Focus first creates the attention to detail that's critical in battle. A quarterback in a huddle, a pitcher and a catcher both embody focus. If you look at the right thing, you stand a better chance of reacting the right way.
>
> When you're at the highest point in the world at what you do, the only way you can be better than your opponent is to have instincts – *anticipation.* Instinctive behavior sets you apart in battle. During the week, I'm encouraging my players to play with instincts and anticipation so they'll be better than anybody else on game day. It all starts with focus and attention to detail.
>
> Communication has to be heard to be effective. More important than hearing me is feeling me. Changing the environment in the room affects the 'feel.' When you get all five senses engaged, people embody your message, and it becomes their message.

Rules of Engagement. Coach Williams says, "When you see a lack of focus or attentiveness, the solution to engagement and buy in is getting your people to talk. Ego is the single most powerful narcotic in the world."

- Define the rules of engagement – just because you have a headset doesn't mean you should talk.

- Don't create chaos.

- Figure out communication – track what has been said; establish a flow.

> *Ego is the single most powerful narcotic in the world.*
> *– Gregg Williams*

- Use/create common terms - use precise words with an agreed-on meaning.

- Be clear - stay mission specific - no repetition - no assumptions.

- No ego or separation of power. Keep an eye on the ultimate goal.

CHAPTER 48

COMMUNICATION AND CONGRUENCE

Our body language, paralanguage, and content have to be congruent. Any misalignment between these factors reduces credibility and effectiveness. "Effortless" takes effort.

Consistent congruency creates credibility. Misalignment reduces credibility and effectiveness.

Giving Constructive Criticism – The Sandwich Technique. The sandwich technique got a bad rap when it was first introduced because it was misused. The strategy is to sandwich constructive criticism with a positive statement before and after the criticism. However, when people first used this technique, it came off as patronizing and insincere, creating the opposite of the intended effect. People chose positive statements of identification to place on either side of the criticism, like, "You're smart, but you need to fix these spelling errors on your exams. You are smarter than that." This caused the listener to distrust the critic, because they were told they were smart, but also shown all their errors.

The sandwich technique can be used or perceived as an insincere attempt to influence and even control others' behavior. Reframed, the sandwich technique can be the best way to give constructive criticism if the first positive focuses on something the person is doing correctly, even if it's just their effort. Then, give the constructive direction and finish with the positive results they could achieve if they make the correction.

For example, we might say, "I can see you're working really hard at this. If you can make these few adjustments, just imagine how much better you'll be moving forward."

Other effective ways to provide constructive criticism:

- Tell our people they are *acting* some way, not that they *are* some way.

- Ask questions without being condescending to lead them to the answer (Socratic method - asking thoughtful questions to explore possibilities in depth)[56]

- Finish with the end in mind or focus on their potential

- Never humiliate

- Never use sarcasm (word etymology: gnash the teeth; speak bitterly) or humiliation. Joking around is one thing, but humor at the expense of someone else is painful and can lead to coaching scars.

When to say things. Sometimes *when* we say something is even more important than *what* we are saying. We can learn to ask ourselves, "Is now the right time to give this advice/criticism?"

Timing is everything. We can learn to choose our words and their timing wisely. Used wisely, timing maximizes impact.

Timing is a learned art that will improve as we continually observe our interactions and their outcomes. Long pauses can increase dramatic effect. Silence marinates emotion. Sometimes not speaking has even more of an impact on someone than verbally critiquing them does. They probably already know how they need to improve, and our silence can acknowledge that with appropriate eye contact. Can we let our eyes do the talking for us?

This is why I will never wear sunglasses as a coach. I can coach with my eyes and convey so much information that way. Don't cover your best weapon. Use your eye contact. Know your power, and know your tendencies. Do you tend to avoid eye contact when talking to other people, or look away? Eye contact says so much.

What not to say. Saying, "Are you done yet?" creates a wall. Whatever is said next is an attempt to block what we're saying. It creates an atmosphere of defensiveness and judgment.

Know your power. If we know our projected natural persona, we can use the reciprocal tone, posture, eyes, or loudness to create impact. Proper timing is imperative. For example, I know I'm verbose, dominating, and big. If I lean in and speak quietly, it calls attention to what I'm saying because it's noticeably different than how I normally communicate.

Be memorable. "Information sticks more if it deviates from the norm enough to grab our attention," says executive management consultant John Villanueva. "We hear something as 'new' if it's said in a different way or from an unexpected source."

Who should this message come from? You may have heard the phrase, actually a biblical quote, "A prophet is not without honor, except in his hometown and among his relatives and in his own household."[57] A prophet (someone who speaks uncompromising truth) is not welcomed or honored by people who, while they may need to hear the prophet's truth, aren't willing to receive it. People under duress are often insecure, looking for support or justification of their own position.[58]

Subordinate ego to purpose. "One of the most essential skills in parenting, coaching, and leading is this: being able to identify when you're not the right voice," says John Villanueva. "Sometimes our message is more effective when someone else delivers it. We can learn to leverage others' influence to help improve greatness in others. Who do your people admire? What is their relationship? As parents, we play multiple roles in our kids' lives. Coaches play a different role. We can learn to use our leverage with others to influence our people indirectly, recognizing that good counsel can come from other sources."

"If I understand you correctly." Learning to communicate effectively means learning to listen effectively. People hear things differently than we intend to say them, and we hear things differently than others may intend to say them. When we're more aware of the importance of clear communication, we can strengthen our willingness to try and understand each other.

A single, simple phrase promotes active listening. When we say to the person who is speaking to us, "If I hear you correctly, you're saying..." and then repeat back what we think the other person said, that single phrase lays the groundwork for intentional connection and clarity. Try it in your daily interactions, and see what the results reveal.

"Communication is a lifelong practice," says Josh Grapski. "When we listen effectively, we become more aware of the importance of communication, patience, and a willingness to try and understand each other. It moves us from reacting to initiating, an important step forward in being an effective everyday coach."

CHAPTER 49

CARE

C.A.R.E. "You can't fake caring – you either care for people or you don't," says Jake Zweig, retired U.S. Navy Seal, currently Director of Player Development, University of Illinois at Urbana-Champaign. He previously coached football at University of Maryland, Catholic University of America, University of New Hampshire, Bryant University, University of the Incarnate Word, and University of Findlay. How do we define, identify, and encourage leadership in our people? By the way we show that we care. The letters C.A.R.E. form a useful acronym.

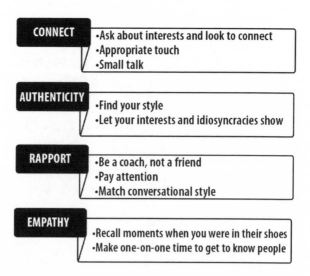

C.A.R.E.

CONNECT
- Ask about interests and look to connect
- Appropriate touch
- Small talk

AUTHENTICITY
- Find your style
- Let your interests and idiosyncracies show

RAPPORT
- Be a coach, not a friend
- Pay attention
- Match conversational style

EMPATHY
- Recall moments when you were in their shoes
- Make one-on-one time to get to know people

Connect:

- Ask about interests and always find ways to connect or identify with others.

- Appropriate touch. Be aware of professional courtesy, but also look for appropriate ways to touch within those bounds because it creates connection. One elementary school teacher greets her students at the door with a hug, handshake, or dance move. Her students select their choice of greeting style from a pictorial chart on the wall by her door.

- As a strength and conditioning coach, I sometimes ask permission to adjust someone's leg or put my hand on the small of their back. It's better to respect the spectrum of how people prefer to be touched, or not touched. Asking before touching shows someone you value where they come from and demonstrates care.

- Small talk. It's not the words, it's the community happening around this act of engagement. Be willing to participate while still being true to yourself.

- Shared laughter is a means of everyday casual connection. Studies show that while laughter makes us feel good, shared laughter may communicate to others that we have a similar worldview, which strengthens our relationships.[59] One important thing to remember: while shared laughter connects us, sarcasm alienates.

Authenticity:

- Find your style.

- Let your interests and idiosyncrasies show. Do you play an instrument? Like to cook? Have a funny tendency or habit? Embracing these interests and tendencies is another way of building connection. If you're the butt of a joke, that's actually good, because comedy means people are paying attention.

Rapport:

- Different from connecting, this is how we interact on a daily basis.

- Be a coach, not a friend. Ask how their day was, how school was, tell me a story...create connection.

- Pay attention. Be an active listener.

- Match conversational style.

Empathy:

- Recall moments when you were in their shoes. Go back to that, even for 10 seconds. If you're coaching 10 year olds, what was important to you then? What did you pay attention to when you were in your people's shoes?

- Make one on one time to get to know players. Walk a mile in someone else's shoes. People will open up one on one like they never would in a group setting.

- As you ascend the leadership ladder, remember what was important to you when you were stationed at the lower rungs. What captured your attention? What would you tell your younger self and why? How would you have received this information then?

We all have leaders and coaches we admire. We think, "I should be more like them because I really like how they handle those situations." While it's valuable to observe and learn from the leaders we respect, we should never try to be them. We need to create our unique style and emulate their techniques that fit our own leadership persona.

As everyday coaches, we will make mistakes. It's essential that we not give up, that we keep practicing. What is our idea of success as a coach, parent, or leader? Cedric King says, "To be a great leader, you have to be a great leader of you. You need to *be* who you *see*. So we make mistakes. Our mistakes aren't who we are! Our identity is who we are. Our role is what we do. We need to be the people we say we are, because life will test us."

Coach Williams says, "Total buy-in comes when people understand you feel what they're going through. It creates empathy. It's one thing to watch the film, but can you feel it? When someone else adopts your idea as their own, that's empowerment. That's buy-in. Buy-in creates a will to win. Our hearts and minds are more powerful than our bodies. Recruit buy-in by painting a picture of it. Show your players buy-in by using them to illustrate what you're learning."

"When someone comes to you with a question, ask them what they would do," says Coach Doherty. "You have to be comfortable not having all the answers. Without input, morale suffers, fatigue sets in, and people leave."

The Importance of Confidence. How do we build confidence in ourselves and others? "Pull, don't push," advises Coach Doherty. "Build confidence by remembering and highlighting past successes. Mine for the truth. The truth may actually be a lack of self-confidence."

John Villanueva shares the story of his daughter, who was running track, determined to shave time off her performance. "How do we bolster confidence?" John asks. "Sometimes the issue is confidence, not physical strategy or stamina." He continued to time her races, stopwatch in hand, never pressing the button as she ran. Instead, when she looked at him for feedback at the end of the race, he said, "You're getting it! Every time you're just that little bit faster! Keep after it!" That encouragement gave his daughter the confidence she needed to actually improve her speed.

CHAPTER 50

TECHNIQUE

Many of us think that everyday coaching, especially concerning athletes, starts with technique, or at least leans heavily on it. We talk about offense, defense, and position skills including biomechanics, motor learning, skill development, bioenergetics, periodization, psychology, Newtonian physics. However, while technique is important, it succeeds only when it's emphasized in its proper order within the hierarchy of coaching success.

"When it comes to technique, people are looking for a 'how to' to copy," says John Villanueva. "Self-help titles talk more about what we're supposed to do and not who we are. Without first knowing who we are, technique is meaningless."

As everyday coaches, we know technique comes from inside our people. Our job is to facilitate our people's ability to figure out their own technique. Not telling people "how to," but showing them how to discover their own best technique. As leaders, we facilitate the success of others. We inventory their skills, and enhance what's there and make it better.

Technique has two parts: 1 – practice (methodology), and 2 – person. Technique without character is meaningless. The X factor in technique is the chemistry between people. It engenders trust, instills confidence, and makes people feel as if they're capable of performing beyond their self-imposed limitations or limitations society places on them. Technique is meaningless unless you're the right person to endorse it, embrace it, and teach it to someone else.

"Imagine we're having a meal at a fine restaurant prepared by a five-star chef, served in great company," says Villanueva. "The meal tastes delicious. However, if we're at the same restaurant eating the same food and we're in bad company, the food won't taste as good. The chemistry between us affects how we perceive the world and how the world perceives us."

—Can you think of an instance in which the "X Factor" chemistry between people affected your perception of events?

How does character affect the technique of our leadership? We become very vested emotionally and psychologically in the people around us. We trust the counsel of people who want to see us succeed. The end result is valuable advice that produces something good. We overcome emotional blocks that form psychological limitations. That's powerful because it's not something you can instill in five minutes. It requires an emotional relationship and an aptitude for what's possible.

The attitudes we bring, the perceived expectations from society, and our expectations of others make us either rise or fall. For instance, there was a study done involving two teachers in different classrooms. One teacher, an average teacher with a class of average students, was told she was extraordinary and was being assigned a class of gifted students destined for greatness. The other teacher, an exceptional teacher, was told she was an "okay" teacher with a class of ordinary students, and was advised to push them but not to expect too much.

The first teacher really was average, with average students. The second teacher was exceptional, with gifted students. However, the performance of the first teacher and her students blew everyone away. By contrast, the performance of the second teacher and her students was underwhelming. Perception, whether real or imagined, impacts our performance and everything about us, emotional, physical, and spiritual.

This is why building trust is so important. Our people need to trust our judgment and respect our words. As everyday coaches, we build an intimacy of emotions understood but not spoken. That trust allows us to influence our people to perform in ways they've never performed before.

As a foreign affairs consultant, I worked with six to seven countries all with their own unique culture, economy, religion, and language. I hired people who understood these countries' specific cultures and trusted their knowledge and skills to provide me with good analysis. I wasn't doing their job for them; I was creating an environment linking the relationships and putting them in settings where they could cultivate their craft and better perform. My job as a leader is to recognize the individual that has a basic set of skills or core competencies and is teachable and open to learning and experiencing the world in a different way.

—*Have you ever experienced the "intimacy of emotions" on a team or among a group of friends or colleagues? How did it affect the shared trust?*

When it comes to technique, our goal isn't exact repetition of motions and skills. Instead, our goal is to learn techniques that allow us to achieve the goals we want over time. Repetition is the mother of the skill. Here is the real magic in everyday coaching: rather than telling people what to do, our job is to know the right questions to ask. Questions like:

- Are there techniques I'm employing that I should reconsider?

- How did we get here? What techniques did we use?

- What's working, and what can be better?

- Is there really only one right way to do this?

That last question is actually a trick question. There is never only one right way. Actor, director, martial artist, instructor and philosopher Bruce Lee refers to Jeet Kune Do – the way of no way.[60] Realizing this opens an enormous universe of possibility and allows us to know our own power as well as the power of our people.

The Art of Delivery. Motor learning and motor execution are very different. For example, we fly planes without pilots because we understand the laws of physics. We base our strategies on Newtonian physics. The delivery becomes the art in the technique, and we adjust to the nuances of the individual.

The Importance of Process. Colonel Greg Gadson, U.S. Army (ret.), served as Garrison Commander, Fort Belvoir. He is also a bilateral above-the-knee amputee due to injuries sustained while serving as Commander of the 2nd Battalion, 32nd Field Artillery in Iraq. Colonel Gadson is an actor, entrepreneur, speaker, and managing partner of Patriot Strategies, LLC. He says,

> We benefit most from less focus on results, and more focus on process. One, have I put the work in? Have I executed the technique correctly? And two, no excuses (conditions or limitations) – you can overcome these. We are here to achieve a standard.
>
> The military has a METAL – a mission-essential task list. Sub-tasks allow proficiency in critical tasks. They help us learn techniques that help us execute successfully.

What makes process successful? Two key elements: intention, and attention. Intention describes our intensity or focus. Attention speaks to being present. Where is our mind? Does attention drive intention? Or vice versa? "There are no big moments," says Colonel Gadson.

> There are just moments. You've heard it said that someone is bringing their A game. What other game would you bring? There is no other standard but excellence, and great teams know this. The standards don't change when people come and go.

One thing to remember about standards of excellence: don't have too many. Have a maximum of three to five priorities. In football, you have six special teams plus the offense and defense. How do you create collective goals? My former football coach, Coach Young, had these objectives: make the first down. Win the turnover battle. Win sudden change.

When people understand how things fit together and trust each other, that's a team. Stay in your lane and focus on what you're responsible for. When pressure builds, stick together. Be present. Be your best, and be at peace. Accept both losses and victories knowing it's not about results. It's about perspective, and that's a gift we can share. It's part of our responsibility.

CHAPTER 51

STRATEGY

Which is the best scheme or strategy in football? Air Raid, West Coast Offense, 4-4 Defense, Wing-T, Pro-J, 3-3 Stack? The correct answer: all of the above, and none of the above. The best strategy brings everything together, yet it's least important.

Tenets for an effective scheme. All schemes, primarily sports-related, but also in life, come down to a matter of time, space, and numbers. Effective schemes are clearly described and illustrated. The success of any scheme is determined by the depth of understanding of the people whose job it is to execute the scheme or strategy. To that end, less is more. No play beats every play. As long as you have these tenets in place, your scheme will be successful.

This is so important it bears repeating: *the people we're coaching or leading are the ones who make our strategy successful.* Most people approach this backwards. It's not about the plays or techniques; it's about knowing strategy.

A famous Bruce Lee quote speaks to strategy: "Absorb what is useful. Discard what is not. Add what is uniquely your own."[61] Often when we think about strategy, we think about zero sum – black and white, always and never. Instead, when we look at information for information's sake, the aggregate creates a competency that drives results. Put simply, by studying and understanding something that's complex, we learn how to make it simple. When it comes to wisdom, the depth of that final simplicity is huge.

"Perception is strong and sight weak," says legendary Japanese swordsman Miyamoto Musashi. "In strategy, it is important to see distant things as if they were close and to take a distanced view of close things. It is important in strategy to know the enemy's sword and not to be distracted by insignificant movements of his sword."[62]

He also says, "Perceive the whole, and do the right thing in context naturally, without strain." What does that mean? We shouldn't look at one specific element apart from the bigger scope and hope to capture a specific technique or tool to apply to every possible scenario. There's always a big picture, and within that, we can determine what to do from moment to moment. Strategy is not simply following a list of rules and hoping for the best outcome.

The people we're coaching or leading are the ones who make our strategy successful.

It's the vision, in Musashi's words, to see the big picture as if it were close up and to have a broader view of how immediate individual details and situations fit into the whole.

—What does it mean to you to 'perceive the whole, and do the right thing in context naturally, without strain?' Have you experienced this in your life? How have you described or qualified it?

—Agree or disagree: We have to know the rules in order to break them. What does that mean to you, and why?

How do you cultivate belief? Believe in our purpose AND our preparation. We have to put in the work before we can achieve success as everyday coaches. Simply reading about something isn't enough. We must apply the ideas.

Nurturing = love and toughness: building up confidence through toughness and sacrifice. That's the essence of coaching, according to Colonel Gadson.

Whatever we practice every day is what we will do under pressure. This is why it's essential to practice the right things.

In business, and in life, knowing the best practices allows us to implement them. However, focusing our intention and attention on the bigger overarching context allows us to know our place, our job, and who's depending on us. That knowledge allows us to correctly choose, implement, and execute the right strategy in the right way at the right time.

"The art of coaching is a skill that can be developed," says Martin Rooney. "We can learn to refine our art by cultivating and developing it. 'High human' skill development influences success. Keep our schemes simple, and focus on playing with heart. Give your team confidence. It's a fragile thing. Coaching is part science (technique and strategy) and part art (emotional intelligence). In coaching, art has greater impact than science. If your players aren't emotionally driven, they won't play with heart."

CHAPTER 52

PREPARATION

Thorough preparation comes from a routine of success. Being our best comes from rigorous, thorough preparation. In any meeting, what is our desired outcome? What is the tone we want to set? What feelings do we want people to leave the meeting with? Who can we speak to and single out? Who can we not? What are the messages, the layout, the timeline, the structure? How many meetings, held how frequently, how are we going to do this?

Our level of training and performance reflects our level of preparation. It gives us the chance to perform as well as our genetic makeup allows.

Sometimes people say "we're just going to wing it." We can, and we might even get away with it a couple of times. But we're going to get fact checked. We need a plan so when we get called out, we can say, "this is why."

The Price of Preparation. We are all trying to live and stay healthy. Today, we're avoiding the risk of injury, not just physical, but emotional and intellectual injury. But the threat of injury is what brings reality to leadership and success. It's an acknowledgment of our own mortality, our own health, and our own limitations. When something touches our body, it's real. When we say "this is too hard," are we actually saying it's too hard, or is the price it's exacting more than we're willing to pay?

True leadership comes at the expense of something else. Preparation requires sacrifice. It involves putting something or someone else first, and risking that we might get hurt in the process.

Philosophy: Ready! Fire! Aim! The perfect plan, at best, is only a plan, not a substitute for action. At some point we just need to start taking action. In skeet shooting, we track with our eyes, and we shoot where the disc is going. We don't aim down the barrel of the scope. Our visual system coordinates our aim better than our arm does.

Where are you looking? Don't aim all day or you'll miss the trajectory of the target. Be encouraged to fail while you're learning. Get your misses up!

The Advantage of Extraordinary Preparation. "If you are a very good feeling and understanding person with good instincts, your preparation involves looking at your opponent and figuring out how to stay ahead of them," says Coach Williams.

> There is a fine line on over-preparing as an athlete, a coach, or a leader. Thorough preparation comes from a routine of success. You have been growing and growing and growing, and suddenly you're playing without thinking. If you're an athlete, you may be familiar with the zone of performance: reacting and playing faster, tougher, stronger and longer than your opponent. You've gotten ahead of what you're seeing and you're imposing your will. In order to play in that zone, you have to be prepared. You can't be reactive and responsive in that zone.
>
> Being your best comes from rigorous, thorough preparation. Your level of training equals your level of preparation. This is what gives you the chance to perform as well as your genetic makeup allows.

Coach Williams remains one of the most incredible preparers I've ever seen. When coaching for the Washington Redskins under head coach Joe Gibbs, he had two defensive game call sheets. One was a statistical overview of the tendencies of our opponents in every situation and the subsequent calls to all of this. It looked like a massive, detailed war plan. That's what he gave the head coach. The head coach knew that Coach Williams had a very thorough game plan.

But Coach Williams didn't go into the game using that one. He had a mirrored one that had everything but the most essential details stripped away. He didn't need to look at the main plan, because he had it memorized; it was just for reference. He overprepared to protect himself. Things are going to go wrong, and we know that players aren't always going to execute the way we want them to. Players look at the coach and say "We did this for these reasons and you had this ahead of time." Coach Williams covered all his bases.

We're not always going to win, but we make decisions for reasons, and we can plan those ahead of time.

Prepare for the unexpected. Always have a plan, but be ready to change:

- Practice plan

- Game plans

- Business plans

- Forecasts

- Marketing strategies

- Battle plans

- Plans for parental challenges

- Plans for organizational challenges

- Installation schedules

- Clear consistent calendars – making sure everyone has the same current information

Prepare to have someone else prepare. Nobody likes surprises. Make sure everybody knows where to be and when. Let somebody know a day or a week before a meeting that we're going to ask them to share something at a specific point or time. Set them up for a win by allowing them to look prepared and smart.

Charisma doesn't compensate for preparation. It becomes more like posturing than planning. Even the most charismatic person ever can't cover their lack of preparation.

However, one caution: over-preparing can actually paralyze our instincts. "Openness to new ideas separates the good coach from the effective coach," says Perry Jobe Smith. "A good coach, even a subject matter expert, can be prepared to present a lesson or subject. Taking that a step further, an effective coach is open to new ideas, committed to learning as they coach. As everyday coaches, we learn as we coach. Coaching is a learned skill, and it's a practice, because we're always learning something new."

"Openness to new ideas separates the good coach from the effective coach." – Perry Jobe Smith

CHAPTER 53

FOCUS DEVELOPS INSTINCT

"Everything starts with focus and attention to detail," says Coach Williams. Focus first creates the attention to detail that's critical in battle. We learn to look at the right things and react in the right ways. We learn *instinct* – anticipatory behavior. And when you're at the best or highest point at what you do, instinct is what sets you apart in battle, on the field, in business, and in life. Instinct encourages right guesses and allows us space to correct wrong guesses.

Some coaches issue ultimatums. That may work for some people to clarify the situation. Other coaches are more interactive. As everyday coaches, we are always functioning as coaches, regardless of setting or context. We coach everyone in our sphere, influencing others to do what we want them to do because they want to do it. While teaching is a part of coaching, that teaching is only effective when the people we're teaching are learning.

What shapes a coach's effectiveness? Three things, according to Perry Jobe Smith:

1. Who they're coaching

2. Who they are as people

3. What their end goal is

Do you have tomorrow organized? Do you have a plan? Jake Zweig says,

> You only have so much intellectual and emotional energy in the course of a day. Expend it in areas that have the most payoff.
>
> The best leaders in the world empower other leaders and let them lead. By doing nothing, we are influencing others to do what we want them to do because they want to do it. It's essential to empower our leaders to solve problems, to consider ideas and possible solutions and their ramifications. Head coaches fail because they don't empower the people around them. I'm not bigger than the program, I'm just guiding the program. The bigger the organization, the less we have to do. Surround yourself with people who are world class, great, or above average. Organizations succeed when we develop everyone around us.
>
> If you leave, my organization is not going to suffer. The only way it suffers is if I don't have your replacement already ready. Make sure every single player knows the plays better than you, so they can make instinctive decisions. The plays don't just belong to you.

CHAPTER 54

ENVIRONMENT

As everyday coaches, we are tasked with creating the environment for people to come to their own conclusions and reach their own epiphany. We create settings and contexts for people to do things they never imagined. That can be on the field, at home, at work, or anywhere we find ourselves in a position to come alongside others and help them find their way.

We act as catalysts to spark reactions in our players. What constitutes an environment, and how can we best manipulate it to generate a conclusion?

* * * * *

Space + bonds = energy. This can be manipulated. This is why Soldiers To Sidelines conducts seminars in NFL facilities or high level academic institution athletic film rooms. The environment inspires the participants. It sets a very high standard for how things can be.

Why is environment so important? Because it moves us toward a goal: to create bonds between people in a good space to create good energy. Think about the environment created by staging a home for sale, creating good energy for a prospective buyer to envision themselves living the life that space projects. As everyday coaches, influencing our environment influences the energy in us and in our people.

Sight (cleanliness, color, lighting, inspirational graphics)

- Visuals contribute to people falling asleep or being alert and aware
- Clean comfortable setting or cluttered and unsettling?

Sound (music style, decibel level, content)

- Loud, quiet, or distracting
- Sirens, loud sounds = stressful

Feel/touch (room temperature, hardness/softness of seating)

- Uncomfortable temperatures and seats become the takeaway
- Hot, cold, clammy, crowded, spacious

Smell/taste (specific scent, pungency, varying preference or sensitivities, seasons)

- Good or bad, a smell is a huge distraction. Imagine smelling microwaving broccoli vs. freshly-mown grass.
- Scents can be used to influence prospective buyers – new car smell, smell of a home where someone has smoked heavily.

Sight: In a retail setting, lots of mirrors and shiny, reflective surfaces create the sense of a larger, brighter space. Warm colors, dim lighting, and soothing music invite shoppers to relax, stay longer, and take their time considering purchases.

Sound: While playing arena football, an opposing team intentionally chose to play relaxing tunes in the arena during our warm-up, making it hard for us to get inspired to play. We warmed up to the soundtrack of the movie *St. Elmo's Fire*. Conversely, the opposing team played high energy inspirational music for themselves during their own warm-up.

Feel/Touch: When I began coaching college football, the team offices were dirty and disorganized. The first thing we did was clean up the spaces, throw things out, paint walls, and organize the equipment room. We knew the adage: look like crap, play like crap.

Smell/Taste: Every object and person gives off a type of energy. We remember the sense of the energy. The waiting room in a veterinarian's office, guests gathered to attend a formal wedding ceremony, the lobby of a stately old hotel or theatre, crowded gates at a busy airport, a cozy pizza place, steamy and warm in the heart of a bustling city in winter...each setting has its own energy, and we remember the sense of it long after we're not there anymore. The sense forms and shapes our memory.

How does Environment Influence Morale?

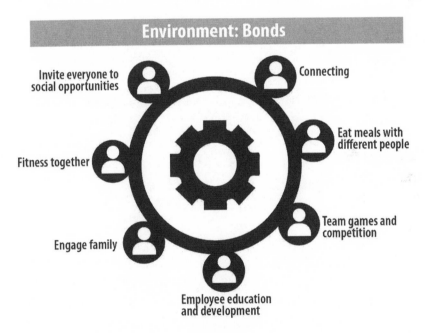

All these things combine to create great energy. In the 1980s music video based on the song "You Can Call me Al," musician Paul Simon and actor Chevy Chase perform a lively, upbeat song in a room entirely painted pink, with pink walls and a pink floor. Two retro metal lawn chairs and a variety of musical instruments set the tone. The only other element in the room is a dark doorway through which Chevy and Paul enter and exit. The energy is the irresistible rhythm of the music and the dynamic between the two men. It's all but impossible not to feel it just by watching the video.[63]

Inspiring people to think differently can be a major challenge. According to Josh Grapski, one of the biggest challenges is getting non-coaches to own their roles as part of the bigger team. "Better team performance leads to better customer experiences and profits," he says. As everyday coaches, we can begin by looking at the standard way our industry or team operates, and intentionally focusing on specific ways to improve the team's performance. "What's the blueprint?" asks Grapski. "What tools do we need? How do we constantly reinforce this? If people truly are our focus, how do we intentionally develop a better culture?"

Cliques: The Enemy of Success. Cliques promote groupthink, close mindedness, prejudice, security, false belonging, and convey a sense of "Good Ol' Boys Club." A recent CareerBuilder survey found 43% of 3000 workers say their office is populated by cliques. Of those workers, 13% said participating in a clique was detrimental to their advancement. According to Katherine Crowley, author of *Working With You Is Killing Me*, cliques are most common in organizations with weak leadership. If you're a leader/manager/coach, everything you do should be intended to ensure those don't exist.[64]

If we get fired for doing something, the people around us are considered guilty by association. Our trustworthiness is determined by our clique. Brigadier General Michel explains it this way:

> The only role of a leader is to create conditions. You are responsible for creating a space where people feel safe enough to show up and be their authentic selves. As leaders, we need to be willing to use our tools and teach things that haven't been done. Our goal is to create

conditions to elicit the best in the human conditions. We always want to realize the value of the other.

Leadership is both an art and a science. Tools like the PDP (personality development profile) allow us to put together a picture of reality.

Our job as leaders is to make the response to the call to action completely predictable. We know what we expect, need, and want.

The measure of a real leader, and an effective everyday coach, is the kind of environment we create and allow. Make our physical space conducive to the culture we want to create. We're intentionally creating a space people can be proud of.

* * * * *

"One component of environment is carefully focusing and implementing nuance through repetition," says Major General Cucolo.

For example, how do you get someone to buy into the program? You have a mission, a goal, a vision, etc. but those can't just be hanging on the wall. You constantly ask people how what they're doing relates to the vision. Making the organization's vision and mission come alive and having participants absorb it. Use it when correcting/adjusting.

When someone exhibits behavior that reflects the mission statement/ goals, etc., we publicly praise them. Correct deviant behavior and let everyone know when someone does it right. Reward the behavior you want, not by handing out participation trophies, but by simply acknowledging the good behavior.

Coaches can constantly, quietly reinforce this message: you've been trained, I trust you, trust your body, keep repeating. Soldiers To Sidelines Director of Sports Performance, Metabolic & Exercise Testing Lab Coordinator, and collegiate volleyball coach, Johannah Zabal, used a metal clicker to reinforce good behavior. She didn't speak because it would have turned to analysis. Eventually people began to work toward the clicker. It triggered a reward response in their brains.

The intention from the leader who is constantly evaluating the environment and how people are responding to it so they're paying great attention is this: the leader becomes the barometer able to steer this nebulous environment, influencing people to learn good followership.

"The thing I love about being a leader is that it involves monitoring the external forces on the organization and the individuals, and when you stare at a group you're thinking about the group and about the individuals," says General Cucolo. "It's fun playing sociological chess."

How do we elevate our team? How do we encourage team buy-in so our people are happier and more efficient? In Josh Grapski's hospitality company, La Vida, he recognizes when his people are "living the brand." "You can see it," he says. "It's in their mannerisms, the way they engage with guests, and the way they embrace knowledge of the company and what it's about." His people are not only influenced by the environment they're in, they become part of the larger environment that shapes the company's guest experience.

As everyday coaches, we witness our people transition from being influenced by environment, expectations, and experiences to becoming influencers themselves. We realize that everyday coaching is simply a matter of harnessing the magic of influence, encouraging our people to recognize and embrace the inspiration and motivation that is always present around them.

—How do you create an environment to influence everyone in the room?

After-Action Review

•Culture is the cumulative sum of everyone's habits and actions.

•Communicating standards and doing things consistently builds a belief system that translates into confidence.

•High human skills are things like our ability to connect with others, our demonstration of empathy, and all the ways we open ourselves up to understand and be understood. Using them is the only way to do something that stands the test of time.

•We can learn techniques that allow us to achieve the goals we want over time.

•The people we're coaching or leading are the ones who make our strategy successful.

•We're not always going to win, but we make decisions for reasons, and we can plan those ahead of time.

•Influencing our environment helps create bonds between people in a good space to create good energy.

CHAPTER 55

CONCLUSION - BRINGING IT ALL IN

Think about a terrible coach or boss, someone who left you feeling awful about yourself and your work. Remember what they sounded like, what they smelled like, how you felt when the incident or experience you're thinking of happened. How did it feel then? How does it feel now? Why is it so possible to immediately reinsert yourself back into that situation or experience?

Now think about your favorite coach or boss, someone who said or did something that shaped how you viewed yourself and your abilities. What, to you, made that person credible or authentic in what they shared with you? How did they encourage you and allow you to try harder? What was the constructive takeaway from that experience?

Every interaction in your life is an opportunity to become one of these coaches. You can either be the bad coach who will leave scars and animosity, or the good coach who has now inspired you to influence others to be the best version of themselves. It's your choice, every day, in every aspect of your life.

* * * * *

If you want to be the best possible everyday coach, close your eyes for one minute, and remember what compels you. What inspires you to do what you do, the way you do it? That is the guiding light for how you behave for the rest of your life. Think again about that favorite boss or coach. How can you be more like the person who inspired you to be your better self? How can you convey that to the people entrusted to you, and how can you create the environment, literal or figurative, to influence inspiration, motivation, and ultimately culture?

You already have the tools you need. You just need to practice using them to accomplish your goals.

Our people know the way. As everyday coaches, we bring out others' belief in themselves by showing them what they already know.

You already have the tools you need. You just need to practice using them to accomplish your goals.

Close your eyes. Take stock of your experiences. You have the agency, autonomy and power to bring out the best in others and live with loving fulfilling relationships in every aspect of your life.

> *People want to be part of something meaningful. They want to know they matter. When you focus on the high human element, in every aspect of your life, every other aspect falls into place. This is how you influence and change society. In the process of growing other people, you're growing yourself.* –Brigadier General John Michel

ABOUT THE AUTHOR - HARRISON BERNSTEIN

For more than two decades, after earning a degree in Economics from Johns Hopkins University, Harrison Bernstein has intently studied the human body, movement, sports, psychology, business, and performance.

During that time, his classroom/laboratory has included:

- Strength and Conditioning Coach in the NFL

- Football coach for High School and NCAA

- Adjunct teacher of Exercise Science at George Washington University

- Entrepreneur in fitness/wellness/human performance

- Speaker and Seminar Leader in Lifestyle, Fitness, Coaching and Human Performance

Harrison is Founder and Executive Director of Soldiers To Sidelines, a non-profit organization dedicated to educating and certifying service members and veterans of every service branch to become expert character-based coaches. Once they're certified, Soldiers To Sidelines helps coaches earn coaching positions within their communities.

Harrison's architecture for winning is based on an inverted pyramid. The largest level, the pyramid's top, represents INSPIRATION. The next level down is MOTIVATION. The third level is FITNESS, and the bottom two levels are TECHNIQUE and STRATEGY. This pyramid model applies to every aspect of our life and work.

Five Point Hierarchy of Coaching Success

Inspiration
Motivation
Fitness
Technique
Strategy

What inspires and motivates Harrison? Helping people, including himself, become the most successful version possible of themselves. He has focused his life's energy and attention on learning the best methods to influence others to achieve the unimaginable. Just imagine! Through steadfast attention, curiosity, and effort loaded with enthusiasm, everyone can WIN.

ACKNOWLEDGEMENTS

The production of this book took years in the making with hard work, guidance and influence from so many incredible people in my life. Nothing is ever accomplished truly alone, and I am honored to share this moment with the people who helped bring this book to fruition.

First and foremost, I must thank my beautiful and brilliant wife, Laura Olenderski, who has encouraged and supported everything that is Soldiers To Sidelines, including this book. There have been times when risk met perseverance and she always championed every effort. I love you.

I learned that writing a book is much more than simply writing. We all need coaches to help us succeed, and therefore I must thank my book production coach Deb Burdick. You are a true Everyday Coach and your sacrifice for our Soldier Coaches will always be remembered.

Coach Mike Alberque was my high school football coach who showed me that coaching football is a true joy and a wonderful fulfilling life. His influence made me want to be a coach, and now his impact will carry forward to every service member that wants to coach as well.

We have been fortunate to work with and develop many incredible soldier coaches, but I must explicitly express my gratitude and thanks to three. Brady Nix, Will Huff, and Josh Adelman have worked tirelessly to bring this book to market and serve all of our other soldier coaches. I am proud of our team.

The bulk of the content in this book has been provided by the wisdom of so many great leaders and coaches. In the book we discuss having one message, with many messengers, which I proudly learned from my mentor

Coach Gregg Williams. You will read in this book how deep his impact grows within Soldiers To Sidelines.

The other messengers who lent their expertise to these leadership lessons include the following esteemed Everyday Coaches. We are grateful for each person's unique contribution.

George Casey Jr. made the time to share his wisdom with us to add tremendous color to the topics in this book. He has been a trusted advisor and supporter of Soldiers To Sidelines which has led to much of our success.

Dr. Amanda Visek has openly shared her ideas, theories, and research on "Fun" which proved to be an integral concept in this book. Her work has had significant influence on the overall teachings of Soldiers To Sidelines.

Tony Cucolo provided several interviews, podcast discussions, webinars, and in-person presentations for our soldier coaches. The content in each of these moments is priceless wisdom which shines several times throughout this book.

John Uberti from day one has been generous to discuss the leadership lessons he has experienced in his life to make Soldiers To Sidelines better. We are thrilled to be able to include his experience in this book.

Bill MacDonald and his family have supported me personally as a champion for the development of this book and Soldiers To Sidelines. Ever since the ideation of the STS Book Concept, Bill has gone above and beyond to help see this to its culmination. Words cannot express my gratitude.

Josh Grapski and his company La Vida Hospitality were the first to formally incorporate these lessons from the book into their everyday culture. They understand how their success depends on their leadership's ability to coach each other through the toughest moments. Our man dates of philosophical reflection seep into every word in this book. Cheers!

Greg Gadson became an immediate friend when he first supported Soldiers To Sidelines at our Influence To Victory Golf Outing. Since that day, he has provided volumes of coaching insight from his football playing days at West Point, to his astounding military career, and now his successful consulting business. He has been an inspiration to this book and to all of our Soldier Coaches.

Perry Jobe Smith brought great perspective on how people receive and process information through the Cognitive Peak Profile. Perry's insights on personnel development and leadership resonate throughout this book and our STS process.

General John Michel has inculcated our Soldiers To Sidelines vernacular with the concept of "High Human Skills." His words and stories about servant leadership and accountability are ever-present in this book and sustain throughout our teaching.

Matt Doherty has lent much of his leadership philosophy from decades of basketball coaching experience which imbues much of his leadership consulting practice. We are grateful he has shared his humility and concepts of coaching scars and "Four Knows."

Cedric King shared his harrowing life story and brilliant outlook on life that has helped shape the leadership and coaching lessons in this book. We are eternally grateful that he has chosen to join our tribe. Cedric sets a high bar as an Everyday Coach.

Martin Rooney, my longtime dear friend and mentor, has helped me see this book to its completion. He has set the ultimate example in my life on how to achieve the unthinkable. I am proud to share this experience with him.

Adam Silva is one of the greatest Everyday Coaches I have met. He is steadfast in his leadership and coaching ethos of developing people of character. Our morning breakfast discussions at the Double T Diner in Annapolis, MD have inspired much of the content in this book.

John Villanueva has provided lifetimes of guidance and friendship for the success of Soldiers To Sidelines and The Everyday Coach. Over infinite cups of coffee and workouts, it has been entertaining and fulfilling to talk through all of these ideas and see them become a reality.

Jack Talley was gracious to share his amazing outlook on life and leadership through sports and his successful business career. Enterprise has a national reputation as one of the best companies to work for, and undoubtedly Jack's leadership style influenced their incredible culture.

Jake Zweig is the example of an Everyday Soldier Coach. From playing football at Navy to joining the Seals, and then transitioning to the college football coaching world, Jake has provided a unique and poignant perspective to coaching that permeates this book.

Mike Taylor has been and remains one of Soldiers To Sidelines' biggest influencers. He embodies the magic of influence, and the success of this book would not be possible without his effort and commitment. I am profoundly thankful for the support and good counsel of my dear friend and colleague Mike.

Mack Brown, while setting the standard model of the quintessential Everyday Coach, has inspired and motivated our Soldier Coaches to be the greatest version of themselves possible as a character-based coach in their communities. Thank you so much for your motivational foreword.

CONTRIBUTORS

The following people embody the Everyday Coach approach. They're all visionary, relentlessly curious truth seekers. Look for their interviews on episodes of Harrison Bernstein's Everyday Coach podcast.

1. General George Casey, Jr., U.S. Army (ret.), four-star general; Chairman, USO Board of Governors; 36th Chief of Staff of the United States Army (2007–2011); Commanding General, Multi-National Force – Iraq (2004–2007).

2. Major General Tony Cucolo, U.S. Army (ret.); U.S. Army Chief of Public Affairs, Commander of the 3rd Infantry Division and Fort Stewart/Hunter Army Airfield (GA); Commandant of the Army War College.

3. Matt Doherty, entrepreneur; former coach of University of North Carolina men's basketball team (2000–2003).

4. Colonel Greg Gadson, U.S. Army (ret.), Garrison Commander, Fort Belvoir; bilateral above-the-knee amputee due to injuries sustained while serving as Commander of the 2nd Battalion, 32nd Field Artillery in Iraq; actor, entrepreneur, speaker, and managing partner of Portrait Strategies, LLC.

5. Josh Grapski, Managing Member, La Vida Hospitality.

6. Master Sergeant Cedric King, U.S. Army (ret.); double leg amputee, motivational speaker, and author of *The Making Point*.

7. Bill MacDonald, Founding Partner, CEO, President, and Chief Investment Officer, Mill Creek Residential.

8. Brigadier General John Michel, U.S. Air Force (ret.); Commanding General, NATO Air Training Command-Afghanistan; NATO Training Mission/Combined Security Transition Command-Afghanistan; and Commander, 438th Air Expeditionary Wing, Kabul, Afghanistan; business leader, speaker, best-selling author, and organizational change expert.

9. Martin Rooney, Founder and Head Coach, Training for Warriors; internationally-recognized coach, fitness expert, bestselling author and pioneer of strength and conditioning; former COO of the Parisi Speed School; member of the 1996 United States Olympic Bobsled Team.

10. Adam Silva, CEO of Black 4, LLC; public speaker, executive coach, character development coach.

11. Perry Jobe Smith, entrepreneur, founding partner of Minute Man Restaurants & Matchbox Food Group (Washington, DC).

12. Jack Talley, Vice President at Enterprise Fleet Management, Enterprise Rent-A-Car.

13. Major General John Uberti, U.S. Army (ret.), global executive and team builder, Raytheon; previously served as former Deputy Commanding General for Support, U.S. Army Installation Management Command; former Chief of Staff, United States Strategic Command.

14. John Villanueva, Special Forces, U.S. Army (ret.); executive management consultant.

15. Gregg Williams, 30+ year NFL Head Coach and Defensive Coordinator.

16. Jake Zweig, retired U.S. Navy SEAL; Director of Player Development, University of Illinois at Urbana-Champaign; previously coached

football at University of Maryland, Catholic University of America, University of New Hampshire, Bryant University, University of the Incarnate Word, and University of Findlay.

ENDNOTES AND SOURCE LIST

Ch. 2

1. Rachel Sugar, Richard Feloni, and Ashley Lutz, "29 Famous People Who Failed Before They Succeeded," July 9, 2015, https://www.businessinsider.com/successful-people-who-failed-at-first-2015-7#a-young-henry-ford-ruined-his-reputation-with-a-couple-of-failed-automobile-businesses-210

Ch. 3

2. Susan Peppercorn, "How to Overcome Your Fear of Failure," December 10, 2018, https://hbr.org/2018/12/how-to-overcome-your-fear-of-failure

3. Mind Tools Content Team, "Overcoming Fear of Failure," accessed November 30, 2020, https://www.mindtools.com/pages/article/fear-of-failure.htm

4. Peppercorn, "How to Overcome Your Fear of Failure."

5. Tim Ferriss, "Fear Setting: The Most Valuable Exercise I Do Every Month," May 15, 2017, https://tim.blog/2017/05/15/fear-setting/

6. Ferriss, "Fear Setting: The Most Valuable Exercise I Do Every Month."

Ch 4

7. Kelly Weiss, "How to Make Decisions From a Place of Love Rather Than Fear," accessed November 30, 2020,

https://www.lifehack.org/496080/
how-to-make-decisions-from-a-place-of-love-rather-than-fear

8. Ross Pomeroy, "How George Washington Used Vaccines to Help Win the Revolutionary War," September 25, 2016, accessed August 20, 2019, www.realclearscience.com/blog/2016/how_vaccination_helped_win_the_revolutionary_war.html

Ch. 5

9. Tracy Trautner, "Overprotective Parenting Style," January 19, 2017, Michigan State University Extension, https://extension.msu.edu

10. Trautner, "Overprotective Parenting Style."

11. Trautner, "Overprotective Parenting Style."

12. Trautner, "Overprotective Parenting Style."

Ch. 7

13. Dr. Edith Eva Eger, *The Choice: Embrace the Possible* (New York: Scribner, an imprint of Simon & Schuster, Inc.), 209.

14. Mind Tools Content Team, "Overcoming Fear of Failure."

Ch. 8

15. Dave Dorr, "Remembering the Miracle on Ice," *The Seattle Times*, February 25, 1990, https://archive.seattletimes.com/archive/?date=19900225&slug=1057846

16. "Miracle on Ice," Wikipedia, accessed August 20, 2020, https://en.wikipedia.org/wiki/Miracle_on_Ice

Ch. 11

17. Ranganathan VK, Siemionow V, Liu JZ, Sahgal V, Yue GH. "From mental power to muscle power--gaining strength by using the mind," *Neuropsychologia.* 2004;42(7):944-56. doi: 10.1016/j.neuropsychologia.2003.11.018. PMID: 14998709, accessed December 1, 2020, https://pubmed.ncbi.nlm.nih.gov/14998709/

18. Manuela Lenzen, "Feeling Our Emotions," Scientific American Mind, April 1, 2005, https://www.scientificamerican.com/article/feeling-our-emotions/

Ch. 12

19. Associated Press, "Marshall's rise from tragedy chronicled, 36 years after plane crash," ESPN.com, December 11, 2006, http://www.espn.com/espn/wire/_/section/ncf/id/2694451

20. Simon Sinek, "The Science of WHY," simonsinek.com, accessed November 22, 2019, simonsinek.com/commit/the-science-of-why

21. Sinek, "The Science of WHY."

Ch. 16

22. Barry Newell and Christopher Doll, "Systems Thinking and the Cobra Effect," Our World, United Nations University, 9-16-2015, accessed November 22, 2019, https://ourworld.unu.edu/en/systems-thinking-and-the-cobra-effect

23. The University of Texas at Austin, McCombs School of Business, Ethics Unwrapped, "Wells Fargo Fraud," accessed November 22, 2019, https://ethicsunwrapped.utexas.edu/video/wells-fargo-fraud

Ch. 17

24. Sinek, "The Science of WHY."

25. powerofpositivity.com, "5 Differences Between Finding Your Passion and Your Purpose," accessed November 30, 2020, https://www.powerofpositivity.com/difference-between-passion-and-purpose/

Ch. 20

26. Adapted from Robert B. Austenfeld, Jr., "W. Edwards Deming: The Story of a Truly Remarkable Person, (Received on May 10, 2001)," accessed October 10, 2020, http://web.crc.losrios.edu/~larsenl/Extra-Materials/WEDeming_shortbio_Ff4203.pdf

Ch. 21

27. The W. Edwards Deming Institute, "PDSA Cycle," accessed November 30, 2020, https://deming.org/explore/pdsa/

Ch. 22

28. Harvard T. H. Chan School of Public Health, News, "Poll: Three in four adults played sports when they were younger, but only one in four still plays," June 15, 2005, https://www.hsph.harvard.edu/news/press-releases/poll-many-adults-played-sports-when-young-but-few-still-play/

29. Executive Summary, National Youth Sports Strategy, "Defining the Challenge," accessed November 30, 2020, https://health.gov/sites/default/files/2019-10/NYSS_ExecutiveSummary.pdf health.gov

Ch. 24

30. Catarina Linn, MAPP, Psychologist, "Broaden-and-Build Theory of Positive Emotions," January 9, 2020, https://positivepsychology.com/broaden-build-theory/

31. Judy Willis, "The Neuroscience of Joyful Education," Educational Leadership, Summer 2007, Volume 64, https://www.psychologytoday.com/files/attachments/4141/the-neuroscience-joyful-education-judy-willis-md.pdf

Ch. 25

32. James Clear, "How Experts Practice Better than the Rest," www.jamesclear.com, accessed December 1, 2020, https://jamesclear.com/deliberate-practice-strategy

Ch. 29

33. Coach Bob Starkey, "Colin Powell's Leadership Traits," Hoop Thoughts blog, November 25, 2008, http://hoopthoughts.blogspot.com/2008/11/colin-powells-leadership-traits.html

34. Matt Gilligan, "The Origin of the Term 'Devil's Advocate' Comes Directly From the Catholic Church," accessed December 1, 2020, https://didyouknowfacts.com/origin-term-devils-advocate-comes-directly-catholic-church/

35. Lisa Vollmer, "Jack Welch: Create Candor in the Workplace," Stanford Graduate School of Business, April 1, 2005, https://www.gsb.stanford.edu/insights/jack-welch-create-candor-workplace

Ch. 30

36. Definitions.net, "Definitions for 'Satoru,'" Wikipedia, accessed December 1, 2020, https://www.definitions.net/definition/Satoru

37. Sarah Gingell, Ph.D., "How Your Mental Health Reaps the Benefits of Exercise," Psychology Today, March 22, 2018, https://www.psychologytoday.com/us/blog/what-works-and-why/201803/how-your-mental-health-reaps-the-benefits-exercise

38. Gregory L. Jantz, Ph.D., "The Power of Positive Self-Talk," Psychology Today, May 16, 2016, https://www.psychologytoday.com/us/blog/hope-relationships/201605/the-power-positive-self-talk

39. Thomas Jefferson University, Myrna Brind Center of Integrative Medicine, "How Emotional Processes Affect Physical Health and Well Being," www.jeffersonhospital.org, www.jefferson.edu, accessed December 1, 2020, https://jdc.jefferson.edu/cgi/viewcontent.cgi?referer=https://www.google.com/&httpsredir=1&article=1010&context=jmbcim

Ch. 31

40. Evan Andrews, "8 Things You May Not Know About Louis Zamperini," History Stories, originally published December 17, 2014, updated August 29, 2018, https://www.history.com/news/8-things-you-may-not-know-about-louis-zamperini

41. Rezzan Huseyin, "Why Self-Knowledge is Hard to Come by and What to Do About It," Art of Wellbeing with Rezzan Huseyin, August 29, 2017, accessed February 10, 2020, http://www.artofwellbeing.com/2017/08/29/self-knowledge/

Ch. 32

42. Adapted from *Hitsville: The Making of Motown*, Showtime Documentary Film, 2019

Ch. 36

43. Gary Hamel, "Innovation Democracy: W. L. Gore's Original Management Model," Management Innovation Exchange, September 23, 2010, https://www.managementexchange.com/story/innovation-democracy-wl-gores-original-management-model

44. Hamel, "Innovation Democracy."

45. Hamel, "Innovation Democracy."

Ch. 40

46. Mind Tools Content Team, "David Rock's SCARF Model: Using Neuroscience to Work Effectively With Others," accessed December 1, 2020, https://www.mindtools.com/pages/article/SCARF.htm

47. Mind Tools Content Team, "David Rock's SCARF Model."

Ch. 41

48. Carol Dweck, quoted in Washington State University Academic Outreach and Innovation, "Weekly Tip: Promoting Growth Mindset," September 20, 2019, https://li.wsu.edu/2019/09/20/promoting-growth-mindset/

49. Dweck, quoted in Washington State University Academic Outreach and Innovation, "Weekly Tip: Promoting Growth Mindset."

50. Carol Dweck, quoted by Maria Popova, "Fixed vs. Growth: The Two Basic Mindsets That Shape our Lives," Brain Pickings, accessed 8-18-20, https://www.brainpickings.org/2014/01/29/carol-dweck-mindset/

Ch. 43

51. Paul Ekman, "Atlas of Emotions," accessed December 1, 2020, http://atlasofemotions.org/

52. Hokuma Karimova, MA, "The Emotion Wheel: What It Is and How to Use It," Positive Psychology.com, October 31, 2020, https://positivepsychology.com/emotion-wheel/

53. Houma Karimova, "The Emotion Wheel."

54. "The Dictionary of Obscure Sorrows," accessed December 1, 2020, https://www.dictionaryofobscuresorrows.com/

55. J.V. Chamary, "How 'Inside Out' Explains The Science of Memory," www.forbes.com, August 30, 2015, https://www.forbes.com/sites/jvchamary/2015/08/30/inside-out-science/#cbc5c3251848

Ch. 48

56. Intel ® Teach Program, Designing Effective Projects, "Designing Effective Projects: Questioning, The Socratic Questioning Technique," Intel Corporation, 2007, https://www.intel.com/content/dam/www/program/education/us/en/documents/project-design/strategies/dep-question-socratic.pdf

57. Mark 6:4, Berean Study Bible, accessed December 1, 2020, https://bereanbible.com/bsb-nt.pdf

58. Jeremy Griffith, "Freedom Essay 10: What exactly is the human condition?" World Transformation Movement, accessed February 13, 2020, https://www.humancondition.com/freedom-essays/what-exactly-is-the-human-condition/

Ch 49

59. Jill Suttie, "How Laughter Brings Us Together," *Greater Good Magazine*, July 17, 2017, https://greatergood.berkeley.edu/article/item/how_laughter_brings_us_together

Ch. 50

60. Bruce Lee Family Company, "Jeet Kune Do," accessed December 1, 2020, https://brucelee.com/jeet-kune-do

Ch. 51

61. Bruce Lee Family Company, Podcast Episode #63, "Research Your Own Experience," September 12, 2017, https://brucelee.com/podcast-blog/2017/9/12/63-research-your-own-experience

62. Dave Nicolette, "Legendary Swordsman, Miyamoto Musashi, On Lean and Agile," Dzone, Agile Zone, February 14, 2017, https://dzone.com/articles/miyamoto-musashi-on-lean-and-agile

Ch. 54

63. Paul Simon, "You Can Call Me Al," official video, You-Tube.com, June 16, 2011, https://www.youtube.com/watch?v=uq-gYOrU8bA&list=PLqDiKwt0apqrHNXjclJoNARboRqK-FtVej&t=0s&index=5

64. Jacqueline Smith, "How to Deal with Cliques at Work," www.forbes.com, July 25, 2013, https://www.forbes.com/sites/jacquelynsmith/2013/07/25/how-to-deal-with-cliques-at-work/?sh=72e9531e7920

RECOMMENDED READING AND RESOURCES

(in order of appearance in this book)

Bill Starr, *The Strongest Shall Survive,* Fitness Consultants and Supply, January 1, 1999.

Schulz, Katherine, *Being Wrong: Adventures in the Margin of Error,* New York: Harper Collins Publishers, 2010.

Ferriss, Tim, *The Four-Hour Workweek: Escape 9-5, Live Anywhere, and Join the New Rich,* New York: Crown Publishing Group, a division of Random House, Inc., 2007.

Ferriss, Tim, *Tools of Titans: The Tactics, Routines, and Habits of Billionaires, Icons, and World-Class Performers,* New York: Houghton Mifflin Harcourt Publishing Co., 2007.

King, Cedric, *The Making Point: How to Succeed When You're at Your Breaking Point,* Grosse Pointe Farms, MI: Atkins & Greenspan Writing, 2019.

Rooney, Martin, *Coach to Coach: An Empowering Story About How to be a Great Leader,* New Jersey: Wiley & Sons, 2020.

Eger, Dr. Edith Eva, *The Choice: Embrace the Possible,* New York: Scribner, imprint of Simon & Schuster, Inc., 2017.

Damasio, Antonio, *Descartes' Error: Emotion, Reason, and The Human Brain,* New York: G. P. Putnam Sons, a division of Putnam Publishing Group, Inc., 1994.

Sinek, Simon, *Start With Why: How Great Leaders Inspire Everyone to Take Action,* New York: The Penguin Group, 2009.

Frederickson, Dr. Barbara, *Positivity: Top-Notch Research Reveals the 3-to-1 Ratio That Will Change Your Life,* New York: Crown Publishing Group, a division of Random House, Inc., 2009.

Harari, Oren, *The Leadership Secrets of Colin Powell,* New York: McGraw-Hill Education, 2002.

Welch, Jack and Welch, Suzy, *Winning,* New York: Harper Collins Publishers, 2005.

Hillenbrand, Laura, *Unbroken: A World War II Story of Survival, Resilience, and Redemption,* New York: Random House, Inc., 2010.

Deming, Dr. W. Edwards, *The Essential Deming: Leadership Principles from the Father of Quality,* New York: McGraw-Hill, 2013.

Michel, John, *The Art of Positive Leadership: Becoming a Person Worth Following,* Bloomington, IN: WestBow Press, a division of Thomas Nelson and Zondervan, 2015.

Rock, Dr. David, *Your Brain at Work: Strategies for Overcoming Distraction, Regaining Focus, and Working Smarter All Day Long,* New York: Harper Collins Publishers, 2009.

Dweck, Carol, *Mindset: The New Psychology of Success,* New York: Ballantine Books, a division of Penguin Random House, LLC, 2006, 2016.

Paul Ekman, *Emotions Revealed, Second Edition: Recognizing Faces and Feelings to Improve Communication and Emotional Life,* New York: Henry Holt & Co., LLC, 2003.

Crowley, Katherine, *Working With You is Killing Me: Freeing Yourself From Emotional Traps at Work,* New York: Time Warner Book Group, 2006.